Bo's Last Woman?

Bo's Last Woman?

Bo Banville

Writers Club Press
New York   Lincoln   Shanghai

Bo's Last Woman?

All Rights Reserved © 2003 by Bo Banville

Writers Club Press
an imprint of iUniverse, Inc.

For information address:
iUniverse
2021 Pine Lake Road, Suite 100
Lincoln, NE 68512
www.iuniverse.com

ISBN: 0-595-26430-1

Printed in the United States of America

To Arlene, without whose guidance I would not be an author.

Contents

Introduction

My life seems like an endless array of movies, some bad, some good and all produced by everyone but me.

If you've loved freely, openly and frequently, you're going to get hurt.

There are those who would say of me I get my just desserts, which, would overall be true. However, I wouldn't trade the feelings I've experienced for anything else. Everyday I get up, I know I have tasted of life what few could consume. I count myself lucky to be alive and in good health.

The women portrayed in this book are disguised in their true identify, but true to their deportment, passion and lust. This intimate look at each one will make you understand why I consider myself a lucky man to have known and shared their lives with them.

Chapter 1

GIESEL

By the age of eleven, I had been abused in every way by my father, including sexually. I always left a light on near my room, so some of it would outline the crack at the bottom of the bedroom door. I would feel as if each eyelid weighed 100 pounds as I struggled not to fall asleep. My fight invariably failed and I would wake up to the same sensation of smelling the liquor and feeling his hungry abuse.

Pretending to be asleep after I did wake up was the worst part. I screamed inside and was torn between wanting to kill him and the fear of him hurting me. The only thing that made the nights bearable was that he hadn't taken me elsewhere to do more unspeakable things.

At that young age I viewed time as the enemy, forbidding me from leaving home. Till then, the light of day shined on him with respect until darkness revealed the black soul and I cried…

My father, a sergeant stationed in Stuttgart, Germany (Schwabish Kommune), housed us four kids and mother in a twelve-room house on Ringelgarten Strasse. Our housekeeper and cook, Frau Fausman, was so tough that if she had enlisted in the Wehrmacht, Germany would have won the war.

Giesel was our second maid…just turned 16 and as attractive as a ripe plum, still on the tree in the morning sun, with dew dancing lights off its soft succulent lines.

With auburn hair to her waist that accented her lithe body, she gave a twinkle of devilish glee with her green eyes that sparked with life.

Never without a smile and in constant motion, she dressed as most German girls in the 50's—simple and as colorful as she could get.

Giesel spoke little English, but having spent many years in Germany, I was one of the few in the family who spoke German. Because of this, she relied heavily on me to translate when she was given instructions she didn't quite understand.

At eleven, I was just realizing how pleasant looking she was to the point that, if she leaned close to whisper something in my ear, I felt her warmth all over, and as soon as possible headed for the bathroom.

Because I feared the nights, I spent my days as close to her as possible…bringing her bits of gossip, sharing my Hershey's chocolate (very scarce in those days). She knew I was afraid of my father and she confided she was afraid of him, too. She drew me close and hugged my soul with her endearing ways.

"Bobby, sneak up to my room tonight and we will talk and have fun." Giesel whispered.

There was a ringing in my ears as those words bounced around in my brain…her room tonight! Wow! I stuttered what I thought was, "All right," and stepped out the side door into the garden which surrounds the forbidden strawberry patch. That's it! Giesel loves strawberries.

I grabbed a tin and in spite of the danger (the strawberry patch was off limits to us kids after we raided it and left it barren when Mom had baked a shortcake), I proceeded to pick the biggest, juiciest, red strawberries the patch had managed to produce. Next, I hid them in the cellar after washing them and picking the stems.

Our neighbor, Sergeant Walsh and family, had fresh cream delivered each morning by a farmer in the area, so I knew that, given the right timing, I could trade Kenny, their oldest boy, out of some of it.

"What do you want cream for?" a surprised Kenny said in answer to my query.

I knew if I told him, he wouldn't believe me, and it would be all over the neighborhood. So I pulled out a cat's eye marble he always admired and said, "Never mind, get me a quart and this shall be yours."

Faster than a dog let loose in a butcher shop, Kenny had his cat's eye and I had my cream. Folding an old sweater over it, I hid it next to the strawberries in the basement under the stairs I would have to use.

Now the plan…sharing a room with my brother, Barry, presented a problem. If I got up at night, he invariably would wake from a sound sleep and ask where I was going. Puzzling thing is that never happened during one of my father's nightly visits and he never touched Barry.

Barry was the spitting image of my father, four years my junior and the strong silent type. He never said anything unless he had to or it would prove rewarding.

I approached the problem with the knowledge that Barry, if completely stuffed with his favorite shortbread cookies and milk, slept soundly. The cookies were hidden away in a cookie tin in the kitchen where Frau Fausman, unless prompted by mother, wouldn't even let you smell them much less give you one.

Frau Fausman was a smoker and sneaked outside in the alley to have a quick one. Timing it to perfection, I sneaked in, purloined a handful, and just made it out as she came back in. I was hoping she hadn't heard anything and would not find cookies missing.

To get milk for Barry, I ventured back under the watchful gaze of Frau Fausman with a bottle in hand and asked for a little milk for my friend's cat, knowing she was a cat person. She harrumphed but quickly poured some into the bottle and escorted me out of the kitchen.

Barry's favorite milk was chocolate…but how to get chocolate? A tin of Hershey's chocolate could buy you five gallons of gas on the Economy (black market). It was like gold. Suddenly, a thought…Kenny. I ran next door, pint bottle in hand, and found Kenny out back playing marbles with two other boys. After giving up a mid-sized steely and an agate, Kenny was persuaded to put a generous helping of sugar and powdered chocolate in the milk. His mother caught him and he told her it was for me…that our family had run out. A statement that later would have unforeseen ramifications.

Shaking the bottle until it foamed, I had it and the cookies with my other treasures and felt sure that I was ready for the big adventure…a trip to Giesel's room!

The day dragged by. I avoided Giesel, not wanting to give her the opportunity to change her mind. The sun lingered longer than usual. Dinner was elongated by the late arrival of my father. Consequently, we couldn't start until he washed up and was at the table ready to eat.

The surprise came when mother proclaimed that she and father would not be home this evening, as they were going to a party. It was quite far away and they wouldn't drive back until morning. Nobody could have given me a better gift. Not only did I not have to worry about a "nightly visit," but I could spend the night with my fantasy. Life was good!

The brick house was four floors, full basement and attic. Oak staircases at each level led up to the next and though carpeted, creaked with the stress of any step, leaving no silence untouched.

Once my parents bid us "Goodbye," I sprang into action taking my bath, stealing some cologne my father liked…it had a blue ship on the little white bottle. I had decided to put on my blue pajamas, normally saved for when we had stay-over company.

Sneaking down to the basement, I brought my treasures up to my room and hid them in the closet. Luckily, the basement was always cool so the milk and cream were okay. Sneaking into the kitchen after Frau Fausman had left, I chose a pearl white bowl and a berry spoon. I powdered the bowl inside with sugar and sneaked back upstairs to prepare my attack.

Barry had been playing with his younger friends and wandered in dirty and badly needing a bath. Before he knew what hit him, I had him in the tub and was scrubbing him so hard he hit me. Giesel came in and thanked me for helping her, for that left her free to get the girls to bed. What a plan! What a plan!

Being promised special treats, Barry helped me clean up and hopped into bed. "All right, where's my treats?"

When he saw the pint bottle foaming with rich chocolate, he jumped up and down on the bed. I told him it was all for him and showed him the cookies. Never have I seen him so happy, even at Christmas.

He kept saying, "All for me? All for me?"

Yes, Barry, "All for you." When you live with a lot of brothers and sisters, "all for you" is special.

With Barry stuffing himself, I checked on the girls. Judy, one year my junior, was reading teen magazines, her hair still wet from her bath. Charlene, the newborn, was cooing in her crib waiting for Giesel to come up with her evening bottle.

This was going to work out beautifully!

Lights out was at nine and by ten, the house was quiet except for an occasional shaking of a shutter.

Giesel's room was a third of the attic made into a bedroom, sewing room and bath. Climbing those stairs with a bowl of strawberries and cream hadn't been the best idea, as the last set were extra steep and I proceeded to spill much of the cream down the front of my pajamas.

As I shakily approached her open door, I heard the bath running and thought my timing was perfect. I placed the strawberries and cream down on the nightstand and was just turning around when she appeared out of the closet with nothing on but a smile!

My legs became weak at the sight that stood before me. I faintly heard her say, "You're all wet, you're all wet. Oh, my, strawberries and cream what a wonderful thing. Here, let me get you out of those pajamas before you get a chill. Step into the bed while I take a bath."

I was naked standing before her with my soon to be manhood exposed. I woke up from my daze and ran for her bed, slipped between the sheets and big feather comforter, and cringed at the thought she had seen me and how small and insignificant it must have seemed.

The excitement of the day and the warmth of the bed overcame me and my next memory was Giesel shaking me and saying, "Put these on and get down to your room, quickly! We've overslept!"

What! Wait a minute. What happened to the night of passion? Never has one imagined so much and accomplished so little. Crestfallen, I moped downstairs to my room, where I was met by Barry's attack, "More cookies or I'll tell where you stayed last night!"

Luckily, I had anticipated this and had saved two cookies. He was satisfied.

Giesel came to me later that day to thank me for the strawberries and cream. She knew how much trouble I would have been in if I had been caught getting them. Then she said the strangest thing, "You know, it was nice sleeping with someone again. My boyfriend, Wolfgang, has been away so long, I didn't realize how nice it was."

"Can we do it again?" I asked.

"Sure, your parents called to say they went on an excursion and they won't be back until the end of the weekend."

Bam!! My brain exploded, my hormones started galloping to the post and I was off and mentally running.

How was I going to top the strawberries? Her only other passion was gooseberry pie. Sure, we had gooseberry bushes, but how could I make a pie? Then the lady at the bakery around the corner came to mind. I rushed to the kitchen (timed for Frau Fausman's next smoke break) and gained entry to the storage pantry where all the goodies were kept. There they were, five tins of Hershey chocolate powder. I grabbed one and fled, knowing the theft would be noticed but thinking only of the night ahead.

Schanz Backerei was just a block down from our house and my job was to run down each morning and get the fresh baked brötchen (hard rolls) or anything else my mother had ordered. For this I always received some kind of treat, fresh baked and tasty, a small slice of Käsekuchen mit Ananas. Cheesecake with glazed pineapple and cherries was my favorite.

Frau Lange spotted me immediately and also the chocolate tin I carried. "Well, what are we up to this time of day, Bobkins," she asked.

I motioned her to the side of the large cases and in my most mysterious voice said, "My mother's favorite treat is gooseberry pie, I'd like to trade one for this tin of chocolate."

I'm sure to this day she knew my mother's favorite wasn't gooseberry pie, as she has never ordered one…but a hard-to-get tin of American chocolate swayed her better judgment and the fix was in. "Well, meina klina liebschi, it just so happens I have some fresh baked gooseberry pie cooling out back, you wait."

The chocolate disappeared quickly into the folds of her white apron and she was away with a quickness that belied her large girth and weight.

Having solved the gooseberry pie problem (hidden in the usual place), I thought and thought about the embarrassment of falling asleep. Consequently, I announced to anyone listening that I was taking a nap and I wasn't to be disturbed. The last time I had taken a nap was forcibly in kindergarten.

My sister, Judy, knew something was up. She came up to my room immediately and inquired about my health.

"Oh, I'm fine, Judy. I just didn't sleep good last night with mom and dad away, so I thought I'd take a nap before dinner time." She bought it, I thought, but later found out that was not the case.

As mom and dad were not expected, Frau Fausman made a light meal that evening, mainly of leftover roast beef, applesauce, vegetables and fresh-baked bread. She had also fixed a chocolate pudding. (Mother always suspected there wasn't half the chocolate in there that was supposed to be.)

My brother and sister asked me why I had slept the day away…Giesel interceded, "Bobby isn't feeling quite himself, so I told him sleep would make him feel better. (She was way ahead of me.) "It helped, didn't it Bobby?"

My reply, "Oh yeah, I feel great but I don't know if I'll get to sleep tonight."

"That's OK," she replied. "I'll let you stay up a little later tonight and help me fold the laundry I did today." Being naïve in women's ways, I didn't know for sure if laundry was what she really meant.

After the going-to-bed routine had run its course, Barry (satisfied that I would be helping Giesel fold laundry) slept.

Judy was reading her teen magazine that had just arrived from the States by flashlight under the covers. She normally fell asleep like that and the batteries went dead.

The baby, Charlene, was softly breathing in slumber land.

I checked myself in the mirror once more, placed a dab more cologne on my neck, and with the fresh-baked gooseberry pie (no milk this time), I climbed the stairs to Giesel's room like a hunter approaching his first opportunity.

The door was ajar and I could see her before she noticed me. She was down to a sheer slip with thin shoulder straps and just a bit of lace covering her breasts. Her surprisingly dark nipples showed through, nipples excited by the friction of her movements. As she folded the laundry on the bed, the light behind her made her hips look seductive and it was obvious no restrictions remained.

"Oh, Bobby, I didn't hear you come up. Well what have we here? Gooseberry pie! My favorite. Where did you get it? Frau Lange must have baked it for you; only she makes them this way. Oh you sweet thoughtful thing!"

She grabbed the pie, placed it on the nightstand and hugged me to her chest, placing my face between her beautiful breasts. The heat of her body against me plus the smell of the lilac cologne she favored thrust me into instant readiness. When she released me, I sat down on the bed and immediately covered myself as best I could.

Giesel laughed, "Don't worry, silly boy, I've seen one of those before. Never be ashamed, it's a compliment that you find me most attractive."

Attractive! My hormones were screaming for help and she thinks "attractive?" How about sexy, voluptuous, sensual...?

"Now get up off the laundry so we can finish."

Finish what?...my brain asked. I was now proud of what I exposed as I stood up. Her nearness overcame me. It was like warm water flowing over my body as I slipped into a tub.

Folding the laundry was a sexual fantasy...every movement she made delighted my eyes...the soft touch as each piece was put to rest. I believe it was the first time I suddenly noticed a woman's grace, the fluid-like movement of a beautiful body unblemished by time and skin that shone with the heat of health. I was beyond lust, enjoying the beauty of the moment and realizing for the first time that the destination matters, but the trip there can reward you in memory, time and time again.

Giesel took me to her bed that night to play (she knew my father's dark side I learned later). She, at first, just cuddled and played but as my hands played hide-and-seek, she responded in a woman's way. Her breath became labored as I touched her forbidden place. She closed her eyes and her back arched as I attacked her rigid nipples with my tongue. That night, some might say, I became a man...but no, that night I learned that a sexual experience could be a giving and sharing thing.

The duration of this episode was intermittently interrupted by strange tingling releases in my loins I had never felt before. Almost vibrations that shook my whole body and scared me at first. Giesel held me during these and explained that as I grew up I would have more control. I should work towards that, so I cold make love as long as I wanted. This understanding advice gave me, at a rather young age, the key to sharing, caring, and making love to someone. When you are able to understand their pace, their needs, their desires, yours are increased ten fold. Your satisfaction is derived from theirs, your fulfillment is total.

Some will question why a sixteen-year-old would take such a young man to her bed. I realized later that Giesel was wiser than her years. She knew that unless I felt the love and compassion she shared with me, that sex for me would always be an abusive thing.

We managed to sneak in many other nights, not as often as I wished. With Giesel concerned about getting pregnant, she taught me how we could please each other in different ways…gentle, lingering, and caring ways that left the whole of our bodies flushed with the success of perfect moments life so fleetingly gives us.

Then, as would happen again and again, it was time to pay the piper. Frau Lange told my mother she hoped she enjoyed the gooseberry pie. The subject of the missing tin of chocolate came up. The suspicions hit the fan and I was called on for an explanation.

I knew it was useless to deny it, so I simply replaced Giesel with a neighborhood Fraulein who was loose and would lie down with anything. My father was pleased and my mother was shocked as I told them simply that I wanted to become a man and had used the things I took to buy what I wanted. Needless to say, I was disciplined severely for the thefts. My father administered the normal beating with the belt on the bare butt and all the time asking for details about how she had been, what she had done, etc. To please him, I simply told him what I had learned from Giesel and he was more than satisfied.

Mother forbade me from ever seeing the Fraulein again, which was easy because she never would give me the time of day. She preferred much older guys.

Giesel also taught me about rubbers, what they were for, why to use them and what you might catch if you didn't. At my age, keeping the damn things on was impossible and I, to this day, hate to take a shower with a raincoat on.

Giesel and I developed some good signals to make sure all was secure before I'd sneak up those irritable stairs and slip into yet another fantasy.

She'd leave a certain washcloth in my bathroom which meant tonight is okay. Many times, it would be when my parents were out late visiting friends until one or two in the morning.

This particular night with a secret Riesling Wine in hand (I always brought something and I still do to this day), I climbed the stairs with a plan in mind. We had always made love in the bedroom…the bedroom was safe, for if we heard someone coming, I could hide in numerous nooks and crannies in the attic (and had on occasion), then escape down the back way.

But how much more exciting it would be if we went elsewhere, and tonight I was already set up someplace else. I had changed the garden house (a tool shed used to store garden supplies) into a small bistro. With a purloined checkered tablecloth, I covered a packing crate to serve as a table. I had at one time melted candles until the sides were multicolored and I thought they were beautiful. The table was laid out with the wine bottle, plastic service for two, butter, gooseberry jam, fresh strawberries, croissants from the bakery and the piece de resistance, liver pate on Giesel's favorite, American Ritz crackers.

I had covered most of the tools with army tarps and had made a love nest composed of army air mattresses and blankets touched off by two pillows missing from the guest bedroom closet. Fresh flowers were scattered about with a candle here and there to add ambience. I had even borrowed my mother's atomizer of "Evening in Paris" to spray the place and tone down the odor of fertilizer. Romance and the hint of something else were in the air.

Arriving at her room, I found her with the soft light creating new shades of red-gold glistening off her hair. Her pouty lower lip was full and rich as she said, "What, no flowers this time, my little lover?" (I hated that name.)

She slipped from the bedcovers and grabbed me, throwing me on the bed almost breaking a bottle of wine at the same time. Her bare ball-like buttocks jiggled as she sat down on me. Ready to play, her mouth searched for my manhood as she shifted downward.

"No, I want you to get dressed in something silky. We are going to the Ritz! I exclaimed.

"What! You know we can't go out. We've talked about that before…people just wouldn't understand." She became rigid in my hands, which were already exploring her supple curves.

You have to trust me, Giesel. I have a surprise and with the baby away (mother had taken her with them as the couple they were visiting had a baby, too), I thought you and I could go out back to the garden shed for just a little while.

Giesel knew how romantic I was and suddenly relaxed, "OK, but just to take a look at what this surprise is and then back in the house before we get caught."

She slipped on the periwinkle blue nightie and some slippers and we were off trying to stay upright on the stairs as we took turns fondling and teasing. Walking behind her, I always thought how marvelous it was to watch such movement, almost symphonic in its grandeur yet sensuous in its swing.

Reaching the ground floor, we exited out the rear door and took the garden patch (a lengthy one) around the garden, through the trees to the shed. What was waiting was something we both didn't expect! Fire! And I don't mean a small one. The shed was engulfed in flames. (Fed, I learned later, by gasoline and oil I forgot were also stored there.) The German neighbor behind us was already out trying fruitlessly to fight the inferno. "I've called the fire brigade, you two youngsters get away or you'll be hurt. Go in your house and warn your folks to get out." He spoke in German.

Giesel and I stood there frozen, our feet not moving, and then we realized how we were dressed or should I say undressed. Giesel grabbed my hand and we started up the pathway with the bottle of wine still in hand, when suddenly a very familiar figure loomed ahead.

It was father! My brain decomposed instantly. "What are you two doing here? Go get your mother out of the house immediately. Tell her there's a fire and to hurry. You and I will talk later…Giesel, I'd recommend you grab a coat."

It seems the army had called an alert that required all in that particular command to report for duty immediately. That explained the sudden appearance of my parents at which, was to say the least, a most inopportune time.

I never saw Giesel again. Mother fired her on sight and made her leave that night. I will always regret that we didn't have time to say goodbye. I wanted to thank her for all she did for me. I later heard, through some German friends, that she married Wolfgang and moved to Freurishhatten near the Bodden Sea and she was happy.

Chapter 2

VOLTRAD

My sexual experiences at an early age both abusively and in Giesel's case, willingly, made puberty not just difficult but downright confusing.

I think if we hadn't had a second tour in Europe, I would have been unable to function at all. The girls I met in the USA and developed relationships with at twelve and thirteen, weren't ready for what I was into. One of the girls I managed to spend time with was caught with me by her mother in what I considered a natural act (after all, you can't get pregnant from oral sex). The mother proceeded to call my mother and tell her I was a pervert and needed serious help. Needless to say, I was blacklisted throughout the community and the warning went out...*Don't go near him, don't look at him, don't even talk to him, he's sick.*

The few acquaintances I had among the boys dwindled away. (First, they didn't understand why I hadn't just had her and second, all wished they had the courage to try.)

The girl-to-girl gossip in the hallways made my life surreal. I was teased in so many ways I gave up and withdrew into myself thinking the good side of sex was finished for me, leaving only the nightly abuse.

Suddenly my father, a Lieutenant by now, was transferred back to Germany. My reaction was positive, I at least understood (I thought) German girls, and so visions of sexual conquest danced through my mind. At fourteen, I would have a chance to be accepted again.

Landstuhl, Germany is where we landed…high on a mountain-top…a meandering medical center where Elvis Presley got his physicals. Located near Kaiserlauten (with a small town named Kinsbach in between), I went to high school with B. J. Thomas of "Raindrops Keep Falling on My Head." My father was stationed at a missile base called Miesau which had no dependent housing, thus, Landstuhl was our home.

Our trip over and back the first time was by ship (USS General Rose)…funny how you remember things. Mother sneaked me on board with measles and hid me until they found out. I spent the trip in quarantine, seeing very few people and I was miserable.

This time we flew…what an adventure arriving at Rhine main airport and seeing the beautiful countryside as we were transported by bus to Landstuhl.

Our housing wasn't ready yet as the captain occupying our apartment on base had been delayed, so we were housed temporarily in an apartment in downtown Landstuhl above a Gasthaus (tavern). When I saw the horse drawn honey wagons going down the cobblestone streets with their load of human fertilizer wafting the air, I suddenly felt comfortable. These were the sights, sounds and smells of my childhood (at 14 I firmly believed I was a man) and I reveled in them. Moving in over Frau Haufman's Gasthaus was wonderful. The bay windows in each bedroom stretched out over peaked barrel-tiled roofs, stopping just short of the large drain tiles and gutters. Allowing one, if you got up on tiptoes to see the streets below, small and winding and barely able to let two small cars pass simultaneously.

With our household goods still on the way, we had only our luggage. Barry and I grunted and groaned getting our footlocker up those stairs and into our bedroom. A giant bed made the room appear small, but it still held a sturdy chest and dresser. A large wardrobe filled one side. I always wondered, why no closets? I later found out they didn't build them that way except in grand houses.

While putting our clothes away (we had our orders), we could hear Frau Haufman instructing mother on the bathroom down the hall to be shared with her family and ours.

The only problem was that the lavatory was downstairs. The bathroom consisted of a large footed tub, big enough to bathe a horse. The enormous sink had large pearl handles that I always turned the wrong way. Above the tub was a strange contraption of hanging rods and a curtain you pulled around the tub. The showerhead reminded me of a large colander with the water coming out in spurts and a large leak in the bottom.

The bathroom was at the end of a large hallway that passed Frau Haufman's apartment. This proved to be more than fortunate.

After getting the clothes squared away, Barry and I proceeded to lean precariously out of the dormer windows. Mother about had a heart attack when she came in and announced for us to wash up as we were going downstairs for dinner. Dinner in a gasthaus! Wow! This was going to be great!

Frau Haufman lost her husband during the war, and as long as I knew her, she would not talk about those times. She had a son who disappeared never to be heard from again, and I was told later that I looked like him.

She was a large-boned woman with hands like a man from the hard work they had seen. She never wore makeup; her curly gray-blonde hair outlined her rosy cheeks.

Her smile was her best salesman and she used it effectively to cajole the drunks to leave at closing time. I never saw her go to bed or lie down…up before sunrise and still bustling after sunset, she had a tavern to run and did it well.

The gasthaus was typical of most German taverns. The stucco with wood exposed beam construction had been built pre World War II and carried its Swiss Alpine look inside with worn wooden shingles, sheep's horns and leather, paintings of woods and cuckoo clocks of all sizes, etc. I don't think I ever did see everything.

In every gasthaus I visited, there always was a familiar tisch (a family table) off to one side by the kitchen, so the food wouldn't have to be carried so far. Our family must have made quite a sight entering the room...the typical ugly Americans looking more like tourists than residents. Frau Haufman introduced us around to a local cab driver, the local farmer who kept her provisioned, the local police chief who appeared in his cups when he stood up...so many so quickly, we forgot who was who. Lederhosen, high socks and big ski boots were the look that was still in, in those days.

As we were seated, father ordered wine for mother, beer for himself and Spoodle Wasser (a German 7-up) for us kids (we weren't allowed to drink the water). Then she appeared and I dropped my glass in mid swallow...managed to get some down my airway and exploded the offending liquid all over Barry.

This is how I met Voltrad...Voltrad (they called her Volli, thank God) was a vision...glistening black hair to the waist, purple-gray eyes with lashes that lingered...pale skin the sun would only offend and a body I have tried many times to mentally describe without success. The peasant blouse with a tight drawstring bodice accentuated her 16-year-old breasts, giving each breath new meaning and movement...the puffed sleeves in a cream color were interlaced with red ribbon. The cloth belt of embroidered wildflowers against a green background emphasized her slim waist above a billowing red skirt appreciating the support of full hips and hugging the outline of her slim legs in ways that men only dream of.

Volli...silent movement that sings as she passes you...as the silkiness and softness that is her invades your senses and caresses your soul. Her first words through the haze of my coughing spasm I can hear to this day. Through those lipstick-less full red lips she asked, "Are you okay?"

Then she touched my back and rubbed it. I floated to the floor, senseless, with a smile on my face.

That first "love at first sight" evening was uneventful after my fainting spell (the doctor said later it was a way of handling stress) and we were served red cabbage, potatoes and Wiener schnitzel. The gasthaus filled to capacity with the locals eyeing us suspiciously, then coming over to introduce themselves when they found out my father was an officer from up on the hill. (I learned later on, there apparently was a black market trade and they all wanted new sources or connections.)

In spite of my hunger, my attention was on only one person, Volli. She was here, there and everywhere, carrying beer steins, cleaning tables and being beckoned by every male in the place...a kaleidoscope of movement and color impacting my memory forever.

Volli noticed me not, even when she came close by and I coughed for effect; she ignored me. She was her mother's child, focused on the job at hand. Suddenly, at the end of our meal, father was paying the bill, a young blonde, blue-eyed, leather-bound guy was grabbing Volli and kissing her as if they had done it many times before.

She grabbed his hair, pulling his head away, "Hans I told you, not here! I must work now. Get a beer and go cool off."

My heart hurt as I realized she had a man...someone older, larger and apparently experienced. Why does the door always slam on me before it lets me through? Heading upstairs, I saw Volli and Hans laughing, drinking and smoking together. Her eyes never left him as he shared some story of that day.

As we passed a window that looked out on the front entrance to the tavern, I noticed a splendid BMW 750cc black motorcycle parked outside, which explained Hans' outfit. The things I thought of doing to that cycle amaze me to this day, but of course, I did nothing.

I was resigned to the fact that Volli, like all dreams, will go away and the nightmares take their place. I lay listening to the night with the dormer windows opened, hoping Hans would have to call it an early evening and I would get another look at Volli through my keyhole. (Kids don't know what they missed when solid locks were invented.) But sleep overcame me and with father tucked in and not liable to visit, I fell into an emotionally exhausted sleep.

The next morning I awoke with that new place puzzle in my brain, trying to remember where I was and what I was supposed to be doing. With the sound of father telling my mother goodbye, I rushed to the door in time to see him outfitted in full uniform going down to report to his new duty station.

Mother spotted me at the door, "Bobby, as soon as Frau Haufman's daughter finishes in the bathroom, you and your brother get in there and take a bath. Use the towel and soap I left on your bedside stand and don't forget to take your toothbrush kit."

Hope springs eternal…Volli in the bathroom; you bet I'll wait right outside the door.

In my room, I prepared for my bath like never before. I wetted my hair down but my white-blonde curls just sprang back up and brushing it only made it curlier. I inspected my blue eyes, carefully trying to detect any of those icky sleep spots that develop in the corners at night. Grabbing Barry, I struggled down the hallway loaded down with towels, soap and kits. I saw the bathroom door was just opening.

There she stood amid the steamy vapors racing for the cool air of the hallways. The wetness of her skin made the thin lavender wrap cling in places like cling wrap. "Oh my little men, I'm sorry to have made you wait…go on in, I'm through."

I can still remember her fragrance as she passed by me; it wafted up my nose and made my senses sing. Her rounded rear under the clinging robe reminded me of two puppies playing under a blanket.

She didn't stop when I called out to her but glided to a lack of movement, turned and leaned forward looking into my eyes. Her robe opened sharing the warm wealth she carried and my eyes couldn't turn from. "You sure are beautiful!" I heard myself say.

"Well that's the nicest start of a day I have ever had." She kissed me, a moist feather-like kiss that brushed my lips and left a white-hot imprint. "Have a good day, and danke schoen, mein liebschin."

Volli became my life's obsession. If I saw her once a day, life was good, but my ability to get next to her as I had Giesel, wasn't working. Helping her clean up the tavern one afternoon, I told her about Giesel and how I wished I had someone to share that experience with again.

To my surprise, she not only listened but solicited details, pressing me more and more about the intimacy Giesel and I had developed. I was so grateful for her attention, I told her everything, including the abuse by my father.

She cried and hugged me, telling me someday a very special girl would understand and love me. I made her promise to tell no one and slipped away ashamed about what I had shared with her and scared she would tell. Little did I understand about the ways of women.

Volli was occasionally asked to keep an eye on us (the children) when our parents were away. My sister, Judy, age 14 thought of Volli as one of the family and had gone shopping and hiking with her. At times, I was jealous of their relationship.

On this particular day, a week after my talk with Volli, my parents went away for a long weekend to Garmish-Parten Kirksten to stay at the Ipsi Hotel there. (We had all vacationed there last tour during winter. The frozen lake with ice skaters at night was beautiful.)

Volli was put in charge and planned an excursion by train to Kaiserlauten. It was wonderful. Trains are my favorite way to travel, besides just being with Volli made me feel more than good…safe, happy and pubescent.

The trip lasted the better part of the day and the kids needed no coaxing to go to bed. Volli had stuffed them with their favorite treats all day.

"Bobby, how about helping me clean the gasthaus tonight after closing? I'm tired and it would be a big help." Volli asked.

"Sure," I replied, "with my gullibility shining bright.

"Go to bed now and I'll wake you up later," Volli offered.

The nights father was away I slept peacefully and fully, but suddenly a hand was grabbing me and I woke up in fear. But it was Volli in that thin robe with the light from the doorway displaying a silhouette of lovely lines.

"Bobby, come with me," she whispered.

"I have to get dressed."

"No, come as you are," she insisted.

Down the hallway, she led me into her room. I had never been inside and always wondered what it looked like. The first thing that struck me were the two full-length standing mirrors on either side of the goose-down comforted bed. They looked out of place with their empty reflections. One lone large yellow candle lit the bedroom, creating and casting romantic, fanciful flickers on everything.

Volli handed me a glass of wine and said, "It's time you're permitted to enjoy something that will warm your mind and insides."

She slipped out of her robe admiring herself in the mirror as she did so, "Do you really think I'm beautiful still?"

My stomach was in knots and my mouth dry in spite of the recent gulp of wine. I mumbled, "You know I do."

"Well tell me again, Bobby, I need to hear it." said Volli with anguish in her voice.

I replied, "You're the most beautiful person I have ever known and your beauty makes me tremble."

Standing there throwing her hair back, she drank her wine and devoured my devoted remarks. Her breasts pouted as petulant lips, nipples erect and pointy hard. The arch of her back was overly curved as a niche for a fine figurine.

She slowly turned as if on a moving pedestal, the flickering flame of the candlelight fondling her skin, teasing me with shadows and glowing with passion. She reached out and touched what had not been touched for a while. "What a wonderful soldier you have, how hard he is." she throatily explained. "No wonder Giesel took time with you as I intend to do."

She took my clothes off before I realized it, sat me on the bed and pushed the mirror so we both could be seen. "Don't we make a beautiful picture? Your soldier is erect and begging for attention as are the nipples on my breasts."

Before I could reply, she engulfed me in flames orally and massaging me and forcing my fingers to pinch her nipples in a hard way. I felt her body shudder, the realization that she was enjoying me made my manhood larger than it had ever been. The backed-up ocean slammed at the floodgates for relief. I stopped mid-stream. It was then I realized my control. My real pleasure was to give, not receive. I lifted her onto the bed and gently feathered her body with my tongue, tantalizing her neck, shoulders and arms. She forced my shoulders down to her hips and let my lips gently kiss her naval…all the while with burning looks at me. She was reveling in her reflection in the mirrors while I pleasured her in every way with a wildness that grew the more things I did. She rewarded me with release, revived and yet again relieved me to an extreme that left me with a prostate that ached for days. Volli gave me that night and just a few more.

"Volli, what about Hans?" I asked one night when we had a little time.

"Hans has left me," she said with hurt in her voice.

"Why would he do that?" I stupidly said.

"I'm with child and he doesn't believe it's his," she sobbed.

"Oh my, is it mine?"

"What, you stupid boy. I was already pregnant the first night I was with you. You haven't figured that out? Why did you think I would let you have me with no protection?"

We were moved to base housing the next week. I saw Volli two more times but socially over a beer. She married Hans and had the baby. Part of me will always be hers for sharing her hurt and my needs in a very special way. She made me believe I could and would be able to be something special and for that I am grateful.

Chapter 3

JANET

Living as an army dependent in Germany restricted one's ability to find a part-time job. Most were taken by Germans trying to recover from the war. After setting pins in the base bowling alley for seven cents per lane bowled, I realized if I was to make any real money, I needed to do something else. Babysitting paid five dollars an hour, which in those days was a lot of money, considering the minimum wage was only one dollar and sixty-five cents.

Babysitting for infants was something I was good at. Babies seemed to take to me and I didn't find changing diapers or feeding any trouble. Hence, at fifteen I was a catch as most girls old enough didn't want to baby-sit infants.

We were still living in officer's quarters at Landstuhl. This particular day, I had planned a ride around town on my new 48cc Meike moped. A phone call from a friend of my father changed all that. It seemed he had a friend of his wife's visiting, a beauty queen. Janet was a striking brunette with big doe-like eyes, a magnetic mouth that flashed white teeth a dentist would envy. At five foot five, her small frame held ample breasts that seemed to pout even through her bra.

I was asked to baby-sit because Lieutenant Catalano had a command performance to attend and didn't want to burden Janet with the baby. I arrived to find the Catalanos just leaving and Janet in a bathrobe still looking like a beauty queen. I later learned that she was only nineteen and had won a number of beauty contests.

As he was leaving, Lieutenant Catalano remarked, "Hope your date goes well, Janet."

I asked Janet about the date and she said the Lieutenant had fixed her up with a blind date and she really wasn't looking forward to it. I was disappointed, as I had hoped to spend some time with her. The baby had been fed and was already sleeping peacefully…all I had to do was check on him once in awhile.

Janet rushed off to get ready for her date and called me to zip her up, which I loved. She had chosen a dark green silk dress that was an inch off her shoulders and in a straight line across her pale white neck and made me want to nibble her. The fragrance she wore fired me up and made me instantly erect. Hiding this condition required me to sit down immediately on the bed…so quickly it startled her and she said, "Bobby is there something wrong, did you hurt yourself on the zipper?" Reaching out for my hand, she suddenly realized my condition.

She looked me straight in the eyes and said softly, "Don't worry, it's only natural. Thanks for the compliment."

Embarrassment was an understatement for my condition. I remember sitting there until she left, singing out to me, "Bobby, I won't be late."

I finally got up and watched her meet her date, a very young looking Lieutenant, outside the building.

Thinking, "that was that," I started looking around for something to pass the time. Finding a stack of magazines I didn't expect named "Adam" (the fifties answer to Playboy), they contained a wealth of sexual stories that explicitly depicted sexual acts and incidents. I had a ball reading for two hours straight. The baby hadn't made a peep, but I still got up and checked on him, making sure I could see his chest move so I knew he was breathing. I resumed my sexual voyages and about an hour later heard a key in the door. I expected to see the Lieutenant and his wife but instead it was Janet, back early as she had said.

"Bobby, glad to see you didn't fall asleep. Oh, what's that you're reading?"

I had tried to hide the magazines and failed as she grabbed it and lifted it out from between the cushions I had stuffed them in.

"Adam, aren't you a little young to be reading these?"

"There's nothing in them I don't know about already," I said defensively.

She laughed and said, "Is that so? Well I'm impressed."

She went to her room and I followed only to check on the baby. He was still sleeping in spite of her loud laugh and our voices. What a great baby! I considered what I had said, (what an ass I made of myself) and went back into the living room and played the phonograph.

She called out, "Turn that up a little, Sinatra is my favorite."

I turned as she walked in and was amazed at what she was showing me. Her robe was open in the front, no bra and thin white lace panties with the darkness of sweet promise showing through. Her breasts turned up with long nipples erect. She held her robe open on either side as she walked toward me, the slow undulations of her hips added to the hypnotic effect. I just stood there, mouth open, gulping for air like a guppy.

She reached out, slipping her hand around my waist. "Bobby, I just bet you would like to dance with me, wouldn't you."

I mumbled something like, "I sure would," and assumed the position which I always felt was so natural. Dancing was one of my favorite things and many had told me I was very good. So, I slid my arm carefully outside her robe and around her slim waist, feeling out for her right hand with my left moist mitten that had to be horrible to hold.

She said nothing about the perspiration on my hands or head and simply leaned into me moving in time to the music, as a bow softly caresses a sweet subtle note out of a violin. My body, after reading about sex for two hours, was more than ready to share this fondling, fantasy and sharing. The heat emanating from my body must have been close to being naked and turning on a sun lamp…that first delicious warmth that permeates and initially just causes your skin to glisten.

We were dancing, but not like any way I had danced before. My right leg was besieged by the hot humid heat between her legs. Her free hand sought out and found my bottom and was increasing the pressure as she rubbed herself on me.

I didn't just have an erection, it was a hose looking for a fire to put out…and then the baby started crying and the fantasy came to a sudden end as I ran to the room to scoop him up, as if guilty I hadn't done it sooner.

She appeared at the door and said, "I'm glad to see you have your priorities straight. Perhaps we can dance again before I leave."

I heard the click of a key in the door and she gathered her robe closed and with a big smile greeted the Catalanos, "Your son just woke up, but Bobby has him well in hand. How was your evening? Mine was great!" (She winked at me when she said that.)

Mother Catalano took over, the Lieutenant paid me off, and I went home frustrated and shaking, yet hopeful another opportunity would arise.

That opportunity came the next day. I rode my moped by Lieutenant Catalano's building a few times, hoping to see Janet. Sure enough, she came out on the second story balcony and shouted, "Hey, Bobby, that's sure a cute bike, will it hold two?"

"No it doesn't seat two," I replied like an idiot.

"Listen," she said, "can you give me a hand with the baby? The folks are spending the night away, so I told them I would stay in and watch him, but I'd sure like some company."

"OK," I shouted back, "but I have to call home and get permission." (God, I hated to tell her that.)

"That's OK, have them call me and I'll verify for you or just call myself if you want and ask for you. How's that?"

I said, "Yes," and she did. Mother answered the phone and said it would be OK, but what about supper? Janet said she would feed me so everything was on ready and I mean everything.

I parked my moped down in the basement as was necessitated by regulations. I proceeded upstairs with great expectations. She greeted me at the door with the baby in hand, "He needs changing. You mind taking care of that while I fix both of you something to eat?"

"No," I replied. My expectations as usual clashed with reality.

They named the baby "Storm"…yes, Storm. I'll bet to this day that he hates his name and probably lived up to it. Storm was, however, a delight. Happy if you kept him fed and dry, a giggling combination of Gerber baby and Johnson's Baby Powder. Feeding him with Janet watching me made me feel good, I don't know why.

"You really love doing that don't you, Bobby."

"Yes I do. I love being next to babies because they love you and let you know it, unlike most grownups."

Janet came close and said, "Love isn't always recognized when given, it's offered in many ways."

She turned out to be quite a cook, the meat and potato casserole was delicious as was the Jell-O parfait she had taken the time to make. I helped her wash up the dishes and couldn't help noticing how cute she looked in those worn-out Levis and loose shirt.

"Well, I think I'm going to take a shower," she suddenly said. "Why don't you try to put him in bed. His bottle is warm on the stove, OK?"

Storm consumed the bottle like drains consume water when the plug is pulled…zap! After the bottle, he happily laid in his crib playing with his dangle toys.

I could hear the shower start up and was trying to picture how she would look when she came out and I heard her voice calling me. "Bobby." The second time her voice was stronger. "Bobby."

"Yes," I said at the bathroom door.

"Come in here will you."

I opened the door and found the room filled with so much steam it was hard to see. A hand came out from behind the curtain and started unbuttoning my shirt. Another grabbed my glasses. "Now wouldn't you like to dance with me again? Only this time we don't have to stop!"

In the shower I was blind as a bat, but after she helped me off with my pants, I was sure what she wanted. My first touch of those breasts I can remember and still feel to this day…a softness that belied the stiffness of those hard nipples. The turned-up tilt of the bottom edge of each breast holding water in velvet pools on the tops as I cupped them together and brought them to my lips, placing each nipple between my teeth and gently nibbling them making her gasp for breath.

"You do know what's in those magazines, don't you, Bobby?"

I ran my tongue down to her navel and she moaned as I gently kissed each hip. My hands found her tight buttocks and those nerves just below the spine in the cleavage that Giesel had taught me to massage so well.

Janet grabbed my hair and pulled me to her, urging my tongue to put an end to her desire. I did this willingly with the water of the shower engulfing me and, at times, making me cough as it found its way down my throat.

Suddenly, she grabbed him, slipping it into her. Fire engulfed me as nothing I had ever felt before. I grabbed myself mentally and thought not yet, not yet, she isn't done.

I thrust as hard as I could but, standing in that position, it was very difficult.

She said, "Sit down on the edge of the tub," which I did and managed to bring the curtain rod down with me and hit her on the head.

She, however, never missed a beat. Sitting on my lap, with her breath becoming ever so labored, she collapsed like the wind out of a balloon with a smile on her face that defied description. "Bobby, how do you know so much so young?"

"I had a good teacher, her name was Giesel."

"You must tell me about her later."

Then she made me sit on the toilet seat and sat on me with her back to my face. Again, she rode and rode and rode and I enjoyed this newly found power and waited and waited and waited, almost losing it and then regaining control just in time. Her body fascinated me, the graceful way the muscles of her back moved in symphony to her hungry hips and the rolling motion of her breasts.

Our lovemaking was extreme. I had never been sore before. The next day I spent trying to reduce the fire of rawness between my legs. Walking was an even greater penalty. Janet left the next day without so much as a goodbye. I really hope she's still around somewhere to enjoy this memoir of our moments.

Chapter 4

MARGUERITA

Attending high school at Kaiserlauten American High in Kaiserlauten, Germany was difficult. We were bussed one-hour mornings and evenings to and from Landstuhl, driving through the little town of Kindsbach in between. My high school was virtually unknown in the U.S. until B. J. Thomas' hit "Raindrops Keep Falling on My Head" hit the charts and he announced he had gone to school there. K-Town, as it was referred to by the students, was your typical high school with sports programs, band and scholastic curriculum. You could major in psychology and sociology, although the credits weren't recognized by any stateside school. (I found out the hard way later.)

Being a member of the band had its perks—trips to other cities, band practices and girls. I had heard that the girls in the band didn't get much attention and if I played my cards right, they were very grateful, especially on bus trips. Although we were chaperoned at all times, with just a little advanced thinking, you could pull off almost anything…to use a descriptive phrase.

That's how I met Marguerita. She played clarinet, was of Spanish descent and voluptuous. A little girl face on a woman's body. All of her blouses needed relief from the strain of those melon breasts, the largest on any young girl I had ever seen…accentuated by a tiny waist (hard to see under the weight above casting it into darkness.) She was short in stature and I'll bet most people couldn't visualize just how beautiful she was undressed. Neither did I.

On road trips, the band had to change into uniforms on the bus. On this particular day, I was in the back changing when I heard a noise one seat away. It was Marguerita who told me she got caught on the bus while the boys were changing, and didn't want to alarm anyone so she hid until we were done, or so she thought anyway.

I told her not to worry; I would keep her secret and watch out for her so she could get off the bus without anyone seeing her.

A miracle happened. Marguerita started showing me attention, making sure she sat next to me whenever possible and we started sharing our box lunches together. Naturally, this didn't go unnoticed by the rest of the band, but both of us were considered outcasts.

I, because of whispered incidents I'd had with other girls, and Marguerita, because she was Spanish, and the other girls in the band didn't try to socialize with her at all. Thus, we were drawn to each other, seeking comfort. Band practice took place on the school auditorium main stage, a wonderfully designed facility with hidden rooms underneath and an orchestra pit that had its own mysteries.

After practice, both Marguerita and I had "homeroom" which you were supposed to use as a study hall. We were in different homerooms, so it made it more difficult. I masterminded a plan whereby I erased my name on the attendance sheet left on the homeroom desk. My absenteeism wasn't noticed, so I could go about doing whatever I wanted to do. I showed Marguerita how to erase her name in the same way. A different teacher watched over homeroom each day, so we weren't missed.

However, there were 200 students on campus. Where could we spend some time alone together?

The auditorium! No one else used it except the drama club after school or rehearsals when the school play was underway. The catacombs under the stage made a great hideaway, and we could hear anyone's approach because of the wood flooring above.

One had to walk across the stage full length to get to the under-stage entrance—a winding circular cast-iron staircase that wound its way down a considerable distance. The dangle of pulleys and cables hid the small storage rooms left and right. We chose the one that had access to the prompter's platform that could be raised. By pulling it to stage level, just below the footlights, the prompter was unseen by the audience but in sight of the actors during the play. You could crawl out the opening and escape unseen…we knew that because I had Marguerita come after me as I tried it. She neither saw me nor heard me pull my way up to the opening and slip through to safety.

Now our stage was set. I found some blankets that covered sets and made us a cozy bed. I had candles from the emergency supplies I had run across in the supply room in the basement and wine that I had sneaked in my saxophone case a number of times.

The first time, Marguerita was the brave one, lighting the candles and opening the wine while I listened for anyone's approach. She was out of her clothes before I turned around, the candlelight silhouetting her voluptuous body creating soft gold highways that I yearned to travel.

She reached out to me, helping me undress and rewarding my manhood with a kiss and then placing a condom, which I never really understood how she happened to have (duh?), encasing me in latex which I abhorred and saying, "I don't want to get pregnant, so let's be safe."

Not only was she beautiful, but she was smart. I found Marguerita to be the most realistic woman about sex I had been with. She knew what she wanted and what price she was willing to pay or not pay for it. Look up the words "Spanish women" in the dictionary and you will probably find "tremendous endurance." With hips that held me in place, she pounded me into climaxes with the emphases on climb…taking me higher and higher each time, leaving us both sweaty and breathless.

She kept whispering in my ear, "this is so good, so good, stay with me, hold on, hold on, oh yes…oh yes," Then she would shake like a blender on high speed followed by a rhythmic stroke as she started herself again.

I was a bystander, she was in charge and this was a new experience for me. When I tried to change positions she'd push me down and say, "No, don't change, it's wonderful this way."

Lying there with her on top of me, I would get a glimpse of her face between her magnificent breasts or when she leaned down and whispered to me. Marguerita was special because she was free. Free with me. Free to explore the ways she liked sex. In the band, she was shy, stay behind and out of the way type, but undressed, a molten mound of moving flesh with a hungry mouth and sweet tongue.

The first time with her was absolutely one of the most satisfying moments of my life and even today, I measure my desire by her. She liked making love to me and showed me in so many ways. I knew now what hot-blooded really meant.

After that first afternoon, I had another class and must have looked bad because my teacher, Mrs. Franchley asked if I was feeling well and did I need to see the nurse. I told her, "No, I'm just tired, I didn't get much sleep last night."

She looked at me with great suspicion, but let it go.

The thought of making love after band practice each day was a turn on. We both would position ourselves so we could see each other as we played. She'd wink at me and cross her legs, letting me get a glimpse of that day's underpantries. We enjoyed the game immensely to the point where our band director, Mr. K. (Never knew his real name. That's what everyone called him because his name was too hard to pronounce.), tapped his baton at me a number of times and asked why I was a measure behind.

My reply, "I didn't get enough sleep last night."

Sneaking to our love nest, we both did stupid little things. She would try to beat me there and undress to surprise me with a nude display a grown man would have paid to see. I would stop sometimes and get a handful of white and yellow buttercups that showered the fields surrounding the high school.

I was heading for the auditorium one day, flowers in hand, when miss Dashley, a spinster-looking type who taught Latin, came upon me. "Well, aren't those nice, who's the lucky recipient?"

"You are," I said, thrusting them toward her arms.

She always walked with her arms crossed, covering her frail frame. She undid her arms, knocking the flowers all over the stairway. She blushed crimson red as I helped her pick them up, placing them carefully in the ones she held. "Why me? You aren't even in my class. It's Bobby isn't it?"

"I've tried to get you to notice me before." I said, thinking on my feet.

She blushed again, even more than before. "I'm sure you can find something better to do with your time than chase me. Thank you anyway."

She then left hurriedly in the opposite direction, the plain shift she wore defining the thinness of her frame.

Marguerita questioned me as to why I was late and laughed when she heard what I said to Miss Dashley. "She'll be looking you up again, Bobby." Little did I know how right she was.

Meanwhile, our sexual escapades had advanced a few stages. We loved the safety of our little nest but wanted something more. So, we decided to have each other on the school bus. This took some doing but the busses were built to carry troops, not kids, so the back aisle at the exit was minus a seat, so it actually could be used as an ambulance.

Marguerita and I would get behind the last seat and feel each other up into a frenzy, then find a rear seat no one was across from. She would remove her panties, which I can see to this day in my mind's eye, leaving her womanhood waiting wantonly for me.

Marguerita would duck down behind the seat back and sit on me. At times, I think the bus driver knew what was going on, but we both were quiet kids who didn't cause him any trouble and being German, he didn't want any trouble.

This sexually fulfilling fantasy got really complicated one day when we were caught in the act by a fast-moving girl who was in my history class who, unknown to me, had a thing for me and was jealous of Marguerita. We had just worked each other up to our usual "anymore of this and I can't stand it" routine when Vicky sneaked back and peaked around the seat, "Psst, I see you two and I'm gonna tell."

There I sat with a throbbing erection in hand ready to satiate its lust, "Vicky, don't tell and we will do whatever you want us to do." *Wrong statement.*

It seems Vicky had some past experience and wanted to participate. Marguerita said, "Absolutely not." Then I reminded her that if we allowed Vicky to tell, our days in our love nest were numbered.

She finally agreed to let Vicky watch but not participate, but I was going to have to convince her. Vicky refused to budge, the gleam in her eye telling me she had seen what she wanted and wasn't settling for less.

Marguerita relented and said, "You can have a little, but he's mine and don't you forget it!"

By this time, others on the bus had noticed our argument, so we all settled down until we weren't the center of attention.

"I'll bet you two don't have another place we can go to and do this, do you?" Vicky said.

Marguerita and I both looked at each other, knowing we couldn't tell, so I said, "What do you have in mind, Vicky?"

"Well, my parents are away this weekend. Why don't I get permission to have Marguerita over for a slumber party and then you can sneak over too, Bobby?"

Sounded good to me and I looked at Marguerita and she nodded yes, which takes me to my first encounter with woman and woman. I had heard about it but never experienced it. Vicky was the opposite of Marguerita, a dirty blonde, chunky, with blue-green eyes and a mean mouth with lips that rarely smiled.

Marguerita got to Vicky's ahead of me that weekend. Vicky had a plan. A bottle of Tequila was introduced before I got there, and by the time I was let into this "ménage à trois," Marguerita was half in the bucket and already undressed with Vicky's hands all over her. Taking two quick shots myself, I watched as Vicky undressed for me showing her big-boned body with ample breasts and amplified by a big butt. She came over to me and whispered, "OK, put up or shut up."

She grabbed me by the crotch, which at the time was not expecting anything along the lines of arousal. Luckily, Marguerita intervened and indicated to Vicky this was her domain and brought me to a handful of hardness.

That night's escapade was akin to a sexual Olympics—each one tried to outdo the other in every way and all the time enjoying each other. At times, I realized I wasn't the center of their attention but just a part needed to satisfy. That episode changed my perspective as to women having to have a man. (True, I was still a boy with more growing to do.) Women need a man only to provide romance, love and support, not just a large member.

Both girls exhausted themselves and curled up on the bed falling into a satisfied sleep leaving me and the tequila bottle both in the same shape. I didn't realize that I had controlled myself out of my fulfillment I was so much in tune with what they needed and wanted. I hadn't taken care of me. Later, the situation hit me. Every man's dream (but mine)…two women seeing which could make love the best in every way. A dream most men have but rarely experience.

I experienced this again later, but not by solicitation or choice, simply by situation. I prefer to focus on one woman and try to fulfill her every fantasy (except pain, I'm not into that),

That night proved to be our undoing, for Vicky had a large mouth and told her girlfriends about our sex party. Soon, I was getting remarks from girls who hardly noticed me before. At first, I thought it was my imagination until a friend informed me rumors were that I had partied and taken care of six women. Denying this only made me look like I was trying to hide something, so I refused to comment when queried by others.

Marguerita and I never were the same after that night (teaching me that no matter what a woman says, you can't have relations with some-one else and expect to have the same closeness you had before).

We still followed our same routine each day after practice, sneaking down to our room, which by now had a transistor radio and hidden snacks from the lunchroom. (I guess we never thought about someone else using the room.)

Sometimes we just sat and talked and it was on one of those days I asked Marguerita about Vicky and why we hadn't seen or heard from her. "Why, do you want to?"

I said, "no," immediately and Marguerita replied, "Well, I can set up another get-together…in fact, three more girls want to participate."

I suddenly realized Marguerita had been with Vicky. "You've been with Vicky, haven't you?"

"Yes," she said, "but I like being with you better."

"Well, I don't like the idea of another get-together, especially with three other women. What are you trying to do, kill me?"

Sneaking to our love nest one day the following week (we each went a different way so as not to be noticed), I ran into Miss Dashley again. I sensed this time she was expecting to see me. "Bobby, aren't you assigned to a homeroom this time of day? I've checked, you see, and know quite well you are," she answered her own question. "Well, what are you up to?" she asked.

Marguerita and I had worked out this problem. If one of us was delayed and in a bind, we were to take out our instrument and play. If either of us heard music, we could escape.

"I'm just going to practice my sex, er, sax in the auditorium. I have a special part in the upcoming concert and I don't have it quite down."

"Good, I have some spare time and I'd like to listen."

Oh boy, am I in for it this time, I thought. Taking my sax from the case, I suddenly remembered the bottle of wine nestled with it. I hoped she hadn't noticed as I wet my reed and adjusted the mouthpiece when she said, "Do you always carry a bottle of wine with you?"

"No," I said, "it's for a friend (digging my hole deeper).

"Who's that?"

"Well, I can't say. I don't want to get him in trouble."

She opened my case, took out the wine and opened my accessories drawer where she eyed a corkscrew among my reeds and cork lubricant. "Well, it's a shame you don't have two glasses in here."

Then she spied it, a telescoping cup I had gotten from a German friend. "Well, what have we here? A cup. Next, I'll find a loaf of French bread and cheese. You're quite the Boy Scout, aren't you, Bobby?"

Her tone of voice wasn't really sarcastic but quizzical, like she hadn't expected this.

She asked, "What other things do you hide? You seem to like the inside of this auditorium so well, you visit it every day." She walked across the stage to the under storage entrance. I immediately tried to play a tune, which didn't come out well as my reed had dried out by then.

"My, you do need some practice, don't you? You apparently haven't been using this time for practice, as you would have people think. Well, let's go downstairs and see if we can find anything else hidden."

I re-wet my reed and started playing the loudest rendition of Harlem Nocturne I could play.

She chastened me with, "Stop that this instant." As she made a bee-line for the circular stairs and said, "Let's see what's down here."

I just hoped Marguerita had fled out the back to the prompter's platform and was on her way up. I glanced across the stage where I was sure she would pop up any moment when Miss Dashley's voice drifted up from below. "Bobby, come down here and help me."

I climbed down the stairway thinking she had been watching us and knew what we were up to and now was going to expose us. But wait, why had she not waited until we both were busy and catch us in the act? She had something else in mind for she went directly to our room, threw open the door and with eyes ablaze went directly to the back through the dark to our blanket in the corner. The candles were still smoking, but no Marguerita was to be seen. The little door that allowed entrance to the prompter's platform was closed, so unless you knew it was there, it was invisible.

"So, no one about! Your signal apparently worked. She is gone."

It suddenly occurred to me and I noticed the green velvet dress she had on. It was floor length and had white lace trim around the throat and long sleeves…more dressy than anything I'd every seen her wear at the student body meetings I had to attend. Her hair was strawberry blonde and some freckles still maintained prominence on her cheeks, which gave her a permanent blush. Cold blue eyes, strong and attention getting focused themselves on me. She stood five feet but looked much taller because of her slender frame. She looked accusingly at the bed and said, "Oh, what's this?"

I knew I was caught anyway, so I'd try a new tack. "Miss Dashley, you know very well this is where I make love to my girlfriend each day. You've been outside the door listening, haven't you?"

"You mean there's more than that Spanish girl I've seen sneak over here?"

So I was right, she had been spying on us before and she hadn't turned us in. I decided to risk it, "Take your clothes off, Miss Dashley."

"What! You must be kidding."

I approached her with a confidence that was sheer bravado, slipped my arms around her, reached up and kissed her with as much passion as I could muster.

Her surprised look puzzled me, "You can call me Helen, Bobby."

I undressed her before I lit the candle so the darkness would hide her nakedness but not mine. I undressed slowly, letting her take in the moment and be ready for me to slide in next to her. I felt as if someone had put a portable hand-heater between her legs, even her pubic hairs were hot.

I had a fleeting thought that my performance might be limited until the heat of her body engulfed me and awakened my body with no problems. She reached out and with a deep intake of breath grabbed me. She took hold, guiding me to where she wanted me and whispered, "Don't worry, I have a diaphragm on." (Good thinking.)

I can't say I didn't think or worry about Marguerita, but it wasn't until a half hour later.

Helen Dashley turned out to be quite a friend. She made sure her day was put aside each week and there were no events scheduled in the auditorium that would cause trouble for Marguerita or me.

Marguerita didn't like losing the day, but was grateful we hadn't been turned in. She understood that it was something I had to do. (Yeah, right.)

Well, I'm glad to say we never did get caught that year, but sad to say Marguerita's father was transferred our next school year. I lost track of her…last time I heard, they were in El Paso, Texas with her father stationed at Fort Bliss.

Miss Dashley married another teacher and went back to the U.S., but not before learning a thing or to from me, I'm proud to say, about how to make love to her man.

Chapter 5

CHARMAGNE

The army hospital base at Landstuhl, Germany is still in operation today, providing medical support for our troops stationed overseas and base housing. Base housing is divided by rank with officer's quarters bigger and a little bit better than enlisted men's are. Basically, the look is the same until you drive through and run into the ones on the golf course for majors and above.

With a movie theater, bowling alley, teenage club, tennis courts and a PX, you would think a teenager could find plenty to do. But I was constantly bored and looking for something different, so I'd pretend to go somewhere and go elsewhere, always afraid of getting caught by my father which meant a severe beating.

This particular school-free day, I advised mother I was off to the teenage club. (I spent little time there, as I didn't fit in.) I headed for downtown Landstuhl. The post itself was fenced and gated with guards who checked you in and out with ID. However, most of us knew where the holes in the fence were and hiked down the mountain through the woods to the city.

Downtown Landstuhl was fairly simple; a big platz or open area, rectangular in shape and cobble-stoned. You could always find a small game of foosball or soccer underway. Sometimes I would stop and play and actually was finally accepted by the other boys as I spoke German and treated them as equals. Some other army dependents referred to them as second-class citizens and treated them with disdain.

This day I avoided the platz and headed straight over to Frau Hausman's Gasthaus where I was always received with open arms. (Volli, by this time, had moved away and married Hans.) Frau Hausman always queried me if my parents knew my whereabouts and was satisfied with my answer. I enjoyed walking into the Gasthaus and seeing my favorite machine, the ten-pfennig slot in the corner. One hundred pfennigs were a Mark, the Germany currency; six Marks equaled a dollar then. I had little money, but always managed to horde my ten pfennig coins for this machine which paid off very little, but fascinated me.

The Gasthaus this day was empty. Frau Hausman gave me my usual hug and asked about my parents including the usual question, "Do they know where you are?"

"Of course," I replied. It was then I noticed a new girl cleaning tables and getting ready for the nightly festivities. She didn't look quite right. Her tight jeans, blousing shirt and sneakers looked American.

I judged her to be 18 or 19 and noticed a small wedding band on her finger. I asked Frau Hausman about her and she informed me her name was Charmagne (Char for short) and that she was married to a private stationed at the base (who, because of his rank, did not have base housing). Privates who had wives normally had to leave them at home, as they couldn't afford to ship them over here and maintain a household. Those that did, lived rough. Char was living upstairs as we had, but unsubsidized, so she worked at the Gasthaus as substitute for rent. Frau Hausman noted that with Volli gone, she really needed the help and Char was a good worker.

I usually did some odd jobs around the place (washing beer mugs, etc.) to make a few extra pfennigs and as usual this day I asked, "Do you have something I could help with?"

Frau Hausman said, "Jawohl, Bobby, you can polish the furniture, that would be a big help."

The Gasthaus was scrubbed and cleaned each morning and the furniture polished at least once a week, so I had done this before.

Retrieving the wax and polish rags from storage, I saw Char watching me. She came over and said "You're Lieutenant Banville's kid aren't you?"

I resented the term "kid" and replied, "Yes, I'm his son. Do you know my father?" I asked apprehensively.

"Oh, no. I met him once on base. My husband had to drive him to a function one day and I was on base visiting."

I didn't realize until later there was more to that story than met the eye. How did she know me? I looked nothing like my father, and her husband wasn't assigned with him. I then proceeded to polish furniture like never before, (in the back of my mind I was going to prove to her I was more than a kid).

Char worked side-by-side with me occasionally glancing my way but saying nothing. My silence apparently impressed her or curiosity took over, "How old are you?" she asked.

"Almost sixteen," I replied.

"You look young for your age."

"How old are you?" (A question I do not ask today.)

"Nineteen."

"How old is your husband?" digging my hole deeper.

"He's twenty-four. Why?"

"Oh, I thought you were a lot older."

Her hazel-green eyes blazed as she swept back a strand of her honey-blonde hair, "I look a lot different when I'm not in my work clothes. How old did you think I was?" She straightened the shirt she wore over her Levis as if to tidy up a little.

"I really didn't have a figure in mind."

We worked on the furniture another hour and started on the bar. Scarred by years of battles with the beer mugs, the bar was a dark mahogany color carved with Westphalian wood sconces on the front.

Keeping these deep woodcut reliefs from wax buildup was a pain. Using large surgical Q-tips appropriated from the base no doubt, we cleaned the figures with something like Murphy's Oil Soap then buffed them out with a light wax (a chore I remember to this day, as it taxed your arms and legs to the extreme).

"You're a real worker, aren't you, Bobby?" Her tone was a little friendlier this time.

"If it's worth doing, it's worth doing right," I replied. "I try to do everything the best I can!"

Frau Hausman appeared with two giant wurst sandwiches and mugs of beer and said, "All right you two, a good morning's work. Halten bitte (stop please) and have some lunch."

Frau Hausman regarded drinking beer as natural as drinking water. Most German children drank beer with their meals, so it was natural for her to serve me one.

Char and I shared a table and attacked our sandwiches voraciously. I studied her build. Her round face and shoulder-length hair gave her a stocky look with the man's shirt collar pulled up to her ears, creating a formless shape through her mid-section. The Levis were tight, conforming to her long legs and ample derriere.

"What are you looking at? I told you I look a lot better when I dress up." She had caught me staring.

"Nothing, I was just thinking you remind me of a girlfriend I had." (Thinking on my feet as usual.)

"Oh, so you've had a girlfriend already, how many?" she interjected sarcastically.

"Only three really that were serious. The other was just fooling around."

"What do you mean, fooling around?"

I went on to tell her about Janet and how she had been so good to me, leaving the explicit details out, but she knew what I meant. I explained my relationship with Marguerita and Giesel, but left out Volli because of her relationship with Frau Hausman. She questioned me throughout this recitation about little things, at first skeptically and then she seemed to soften. Her voice became more reassuring that she believed me and wanted to hear more.

"You're not very happy at home are you, Bobby?"

I sensed a trap, but somehow felt she knew about my dad already. "Well, my dad and I don't get along, so I stay away as much as I can."

"Does he hurt you?"

I didn't answer, leaving the obvious unsaid. I think the beer had given me a loose tongue.

"Do you have a girlfriend now?"

"No, but I sure hope to meet someone soon."

"Why?" she asked.

"So I can have someone to talk to and trust and share things with."

Our conversation was interrupted by Frau Hausman, "All right, still things to do, still things to do." She sent Char to the kitchen to help out and handed me two marks saying, "Thanks for the help, Bobby. You have fun on your machine." (She knew I would play until I was out of money.)

The slot machine hadn't paid out lately and the little window showed it was full. (I later found out that Frau Hausman tilted it forward each morning to give that impression. I finished my beer, moved over to the stool in front of the machine, and started feeding the hungry monster. I did so slowly, not wanting the money to run out too quickly. I reached for my beer mug and found it to be empty. Frau Hausman allowed beer with food, but I could not drink otherwise. She knew I occasionally sneaked behind the bar and drew a little more, but unless she caught me, she ignored it. I decided not to have one and placed another coin in the mouth of the monster. Suddenly, the machine coughed and hic-cupped out coin after coin into my out held hands. I grabbed the beer mug and yelled, "Jackpot! I hit the jackpot!"

I had won two or three coins before, but never this waterfall of benevolence. Coin after coin kept falling until my beer stein was full and still the coins came. To me, it was a fortune. The total was twenty marks...200 ten-pfennig coins!

Frau Hausman came out of the kitchen followed by Char, "I thought so. The Bürgermeister (mayor) was playing that all night long last evening and it was full when I checked it this morning. Bobby, do you want me to change these into marks for you?"

Char asked, "What are you going to do with your new-found fortune?"

"I really hadn't thought about winning, just having fun." I replied.

Char looked at me funny and said, "I've put money in that thing every day and it has never paid me a thing."

With twenty marks in my pocket, I felt like a king. I walked the city the remainder of the day, trying to decide what to buy. Nothing struck me, so I climbed the mountain towards home all the while trying to figure out where to hide my money so the other kids wouldn't find it. (If they did, I would be in hot water.) I found an old tobacco tin, placed the marks in it, and capped the lid tight. I found a flat rock outside the opening in the fence I always came through and dug out a hole, placed the tin in it and the rock on top.

A few days later, I had a chance to get away again, retrieved my stash and headed for the Gasthaus. I arrived early and the front door was still locked, so I headed around back to the family entrance and let myself in through the gate. The back door to the Gasthaus was also locked. As I turned to go, I heard a voice coming from the stairway leading to the apartments upstairs, "You're always asking for money. I haven't had the money to buy anything for myself for so long, I can't remember when. Here! That's all I have, my tip money from last night. Now leave me alone!"

A hard slap followed and the sound of footsteps descending the stairway, so I slipped underneath it and hid in the dark. I held my breath for fear I would be caught.

A short, stocky no-neck man in uniform pounded his way down, "Bitch, bitch, bitch, that's all you ever do anymore, why don't you go back home? That's where you want to be anyway." I had seen the private stripes on his arms and figured that was Char's husband. He found the gate and slammed it as he left.

Suddenly, I was aware of crying from upstairs…deep, agonizing sobs as if someone couldn't catch their breath. I timidly climbed the stairs and found Char with a swollen black eye. She was curled up in a fetal position on the floor outside her door. I sat down instinctively and hugged her. I startled her at first, then she recognized me and put her head on my shoulder, "Bobby, oh Bobby, help me inside please."

I helped her up and into the apartment. I knew the layout, as it was where I lived years before. Char cried even harder when she looked at her broken dishes on the table and floor. While Char went into the bedroom to lay down, I cleaned up the mess as best I could and then fixed some ice cubes in a towel as mother had done for me many times.

Char was crying softer this time but cried out in pain when I put the cold compress on her cheek. A knock on the door startled us, "Char! Are you alright?" It was Frau Hausman's voice.

"Do you need anything?"

Char pulled herself together and went to the closed door, "No, Frau Hausman, I'm just not feeling well and won't be able to help you this morning, OK?"

Frau Hausman had apparently heard the commotion and replied, "Open the door, Char, and let me in."

Char cracked the door and said, "I'm OK, really. I just need to take today off. Is that OK?"

Frau Hausman wasn't to be put off. Forcing the door open, she let out an, "Ach Mein Gott" when she saw Char's face. "That's it, I told him before if he touched you again I would never let him back in my house. Don't worry, liebschen, you take the day off and get better. But he's not coming back here. I phone my friend, the Colonel, over on the base and make sure of it."

Char pleaded with her not to do it but finally gave up, as she knew when Frau Hausman was fed up, that was it.

I had been in the bedroom out of sight but with the door ajar just enough to see and hear what was going on. Char was a mess...her robe was torn, her hair matted. She embraced me and cried again...soft, gentle, deep sobs that eventually made me cry. We stood there a fairly good time sobbing and wiping each other's eyes until suddenly she laughed. I couldn't believe she was laughing so I stopped crying, "What's so funny?" I asked.

"You, why are you crying?"

I realized I had been and was embarrassed, "I've been hurt like you before and it upsets me to see you like this."

"You've got a good heart, Bobby, and thanks for cleaning up and helping me, but I'll be OK. This isn't the first time this has happened, but it will be the last!"

Char, true to Frau Hausman's statement, never saw her husband in that house again. She made arrangements to return to the U.S., earning the money from her tips. Everyday I could, I'd help her clean the place and get ready for the day's business. I usually went around to the back and into her place where she would fix us breakfast. (I was always hungry.) We became close. She talked to me about her dreams and what she wanted to do stateside.

One morning she mentioned she needed some clothes for travel, a white silk blouse she said with just a little lace. She had seen it in a shop in town. I knew just where the shop was and as soon as I could get away, went to buy it. (I still had my 20 marks and some more I had earned.) I still didn't know what I had been saving it for and this seemed to be it. Char was putting all her money toward the plane ticket and expenses she'd face just getting home. Arriving at the shop, I entered and talked to the girl behind the counter. I described Char and asked if she remembered the blouse she liked. She said, "Yes, but it had been sold. (Story of my life, nothing easy.) I inquired if one could be ordered and she told me they were made locally for the shop.

"How much would it cost to make another?"

"Forty marks! And I had only 27," I told her.

"That's all right, it will take her a week to make it and you can pay the balance when you pick it up."

I paid the deposit and left, trying to figure out how to raise the thirteen marks balance.

Each week we were all given five dollars to buy our lunch chit book at school. We returned the book home to mother and she would remove that day's coupon for a hot lunch at our cafeteria. A plan developed, I would use those five dollars on the blouse. I told mother I lost the five dollars, which meant I had to fix my lunch before school each morning. Bologna sandwiches to this day are my least favorite thing, but to me, the end justified the means.

So, a week later I went into the shop with money in hand to pick up the blouse. I had told the clerk not to tell anyone, as I wanted it to be a surprise.

Entering the shop I noticed a new girl behind the counter, "Yes, may I help you?" she asked.

"I'd like to pick up my order," and showed her my receipt for my deposit.

She studied it for a moment and replied, "I'm sorry, we have not received that blouse yet, you'll have to come back. The lady who makes those for us has taken ill, so I can't say when."

The tears in my eyes must have gotten her attention as she stopped and said, "Well, maybe we can find something close to it in our new shipment. Let me get Olga for you."

Olga was the first clerk I had talked to and said she was sorry about the blouse, but she had no way of calling me.

We looked at the new shipment but the new blouses were in every color of the rainbow but white. Olga advised me that pink would look good on Char, but I had my heart set on white.

A customer overheard our conversation and said, "I just bought that blouse in white and don't really like it. Would you like to buy it from me?"

"Is it still new?" I asked.

"Of course, my silly boy, it's here still in my packages, I haven't even taken it home."

I realized she was being kind and thanked her over and over again. Olga assured me it was the right size and, to boot, only 26 marks. Olga said Char had wanted a jacket but couldn't afford it, so I bought the jacket and blouse, leaving myself a little money for flowers from the local women who sell them in the platz.

With gift-wrapped box in hand, compliments of Olga and crew whom I suspected knew of Char's history and hard times, and a bunch of Edelweiss flowers in hand, I headed for the Gasthaus. Up the dark stairs I bounded, entering the room with the key she left for me in the mornings under the mat.

She was downstairs already, cleaning up after last night's trade, so I arranged the flowers in a vase, left the packages on the bed and sauntered downstairs as innocently as a Cheshire cat's smile.

"Good morning, Bobby. My, you are late today. I expected to see you earlier."

"Oh, I had some errands to run first," while putting pfennig coins in the slot of my favorite machine.

I watched Char differently that day as she bustled about getting her work done. She had a nice way of making it seem effortless…her long legs propelling her with a swiftness that was startling yet pleasant to watch. Her hips popped the loops out on each side like they needed to be belted in, but there was no need. I savored the thought of what the morning would bring.

I left a note on her pillow that simply said, "Love, Bobby." So, I left that day before she went upstairs to change with the offering, "Well, I'd better get going. My father's coming home early, so I'd better be there."

I kissed her lightly on the cheek and patted her bottom, something I had never done before. She glanced at me suspiciously as I bailed out the door.

I had skipped school that day to get all the errands done. To do this was tricky. I got on the bus with my sister, Judy…Barry went to a different school. Getting off the bus in a different place on the base was easy; the hard part was making a deal with Judy.

"Judy, I have some things to do today so I'm not going to school. I'll catch the bus on the way back."

"What's up? Who are you seeing now?"

"No one," I lied. "I have a friend who has a motorbike he isn't using as he just bought a new motorcycle. He wants to sell it to me on payments, so I'm going to try it out today."

"Dad will never let you have another one. Don't you remember what happened the last time?" (My dad threw it off a cliff.) "Besides, what's in it for me?"

Judy's boyfriend had been trying to convince me to let him and Judy go downtown on their own one day and I had always said, "No."

"I'll let you spend the day with Bryan next week."

That did it. She agreed to cover for me and tell my teachers I was sick. (We usually got someone to write an excuse to return.)

I slipped through my usual hole in the fence and ran to catch the bus just returning from school. Judy shouted, "There you are! I thought you had missed us and I was scared to death what to tell mother."

That evening after dinner, Dad told me he wanted to talk to me about something. Needless to say, I was scared shitless. Entering the bedroom, I couldn't read his mood as he asked, "How are things going at school?"

"All right, I'm still having trouble with math, but I think my grades will be better this time."

"It's hard to learn when you're not there, I would imagine."

Terror struck me full force. How did he find out so quickly? Who had told on me and how much did he know? I knew I was caught so I decided to tell him about Char, her troubles, and that I had been helping her.

His response was instant, "Is her husband a private on the base?"

"Yes, sir." I nervously responded.

"How much did Char tell you about me?"

A light went on in my brain. "She only told me she had met you once when her husband was your driver."

"That's all?"

"She said she really didn't know you at all."

"How long have you been seeing her?"

"Just about two weeks, but I only skipped school one day."

"I'm not worried about your skipping school. Did you ever talk to her husband?

"No, I never actually met him." (I described the day we had almost met.)

He grew silent, then gave me that look, "Listen up, you're to tell no one about this ever. Do you understand me?"

"Yes, sir, no one."

"If you do, I'll find out and I think you know what will happen then."

"Yes, sir."

"If your mother asks you what I wanted to talk to you about, tell her I wanted to talk to you about your school work. She doesn't know you skipped school today, keep it that way, OK?"

"Yes, sir." (No beating?)

I waited that evening scared to death he would come into my room and beat me within an inch of my life as he had done before.

The sun was a blessing to my eyes as I woke up after finally succumbing to a fretful sleep.

Today was Saturday and dad was usually home, so we had to be, but I found him strangely absent. When I questioned mom, she said he had some things to take care of and went to Miesau (his base) for the day.

I seized the opportunity and told mom I was going to the Teen Club. Rushing down the mountain, almost killing myself in the effort, I arrived at the Hausman's Gasthaus in record time.

The blue and white Chevy station wagon parked at the rear entrance froze me in my tracks. My father was here. I should have guessed, but why? The mystery deepened even further when a voice I knew well came out of nowhere, "Bobby, come on up, I was expecting you."

"Yes, sir."

The walk up those stairs took all the courage I could come up with. What was I walking into? The door opened for me just as I reached for my key and there stood my father in full uniform, but with a look on his face I had not seen before. Fear, he was scared of something.

Char was sitting at her kitchen table looking as if she had been crying and holding a cup of coffee in her shaking hands.

Dad said, "I want you to listen to me carefully, Bobby. Char is leaving for the U.S. in the morning. I have given her some money so she will be okay. Her husband has been transferred to Greenland and will be leaving tonight. You're to stay here and watch out for Char. I'll cover for you with your mother. Don't ask any questions, just do as you're told and everything will be fine. Do you understand?"

"Yes, sir."

Dad leaned down and whispered something in Char's ear, then suddenly left without saying another word to me.

Char turned and looked at me realizing how confused I must be. "Bobby, I'm going to tell you what I'm not supposed to. If your father even suspected I told you, he would do something to hurt all of us. You must promise not to ever tell anyone if I tell you though."

"OK Char, I promise."

My husband and your father knew each other quite well. My husband is the same way your father is. Do you understand what I'm trying to tell you?"

"I think so."

"There are men who like men and women and have relations with both. My husband and your father were enjoying each other one night when I came home unexpectedly and surprised them." (Her voice started trembling.)

"They grabbed me and forced me to have sex with them and did other things I can't mention." (She started crying.)

"Afterward, they both were terrified I'd tell someone and both of them threatened me. I've lived a nightmare since that day and that's why I'm leaving."

I suddenly realized just how dangerous what she had told me was, but I couldn't understand why dad had left me with her until she left.

Did he know she would tell me and wanted me to know or was he making sure she couldn't talk to anyone else before she left?

"Char, when are you leaving?" I inquired.

"Tonight, I'm taking a taxi to the train which will take me to the airfield at Ramstein Air Base where your father has arranged transport to the U.S. on a MATS flights. Not comfortable, but it won't cost me a thing."

Char looked so helpless sitting there in a thin cotton robe. I reached out and hugged her intending only to comfort her and make her understand I cared and understood how she hurt. She pushed me away and went into the bathroom and I heard the shower go on.

"Bobby, come here will you."

I went in and could see her silhouetted through the shower curtain. "Would you like to come in and wash my back?"

I took my clothes off without responding and got in the shower with her, hugging her tightly and not wanting to wake up from this emotional roller coaster I was on. We both cried as the hot water stung our bodies.

I kissed her lovingly for the first time and felt her surprise; "You're more of a man now than your father will ever be. Don't you forget that." She told me.

I suddenly realized I was more physically excited than I ever had been before. I searched her eyes for the answer that was obvious; she needed to be loved gently. The tears became laughter as we explored each other, getting water everywhere and tearing down the shower curtain in the meantime.

Char said, "I will always love you for the outfit and the flowers. I want you to always remember this moment. What you did was done by someone with a good heart. Keep those thoughts. Never lose sight of them. What I do now, I do because I want you to know how wonderful you make me feel."

Walking to the bedroom, I was mesmerized by the softness of her body. The way each side of her rear end moved independently of each other, the muscles seeming to beckon to be touched.

Our lovemaking was, at first, frantic, as if we both wanted to be rid of something. Then it became slow, soft and gentle, exploring each other as if we had never been with another.

Finally, she spoke, "We won't see each other again, but always remember, if no woman ever tells you again…you make a woman feel special. You have a gift. Don't abuse it."

We took another shower, less intimate than the first, but together, soaping each other down, rinsing off the lather to a squeaky touch and toweled each other, then dressed in silence.

She called a taxi and I helped her down with her bags. Frau Hausman, giving me a searching glance, met us out front and gave her a bear hug goodbye, "Be sure to write and if you can ever visit, you're welcome."

The tears in my eyes said it all. So, she simply kissed me gently and slipped away into the taxi, a black Mercedes that sounded like a Singer sewing machine because it was diesel. I can still hear it in my mind…tac-ta-tac-ta-tac.

Chapter 6

MRS. MARTIN

I think it was the sweaters that made me first realize that Mrs. Martin liked to be looked at. The Martins lived in the same type ranch-style house two streets down from us. The neighborhood was just off Governor Drive across from A & M College in Huntsville, Alabama.

Mrs. Martin's husband was also military and worked with my father in research and development at the Redstone Arsenal. Our family, along with two or three others, would get together occasionally for cookouts. The girls my age I came in contact with at these gatherings were immature and bored me to death.

Joan Martin was different from the other military wives at these parties. While the other women were domestically fixing the potato salad and getting the tables set and the men were burning the steaks and hamburgers, Joan would spend time with us kids, organizing games and activities, pairing us up and talking about things other adults didn't take time to do. Joan and I had hardly talked, yet I sensed she had an interest in me, but not the other guys. Her eyes look straight into mine as if searching for something. It was fleeting and, at first, I thought I was imagining things.

Joan was a voluptuous woman. Her short brunette hair finished in soft curls around her face (not really stylish in those days). Bridgett Bardot pouty lips set off a pixie nose and deep brown eyes. All this, combined with a body I had only seen in magazines. Well, to say my hormones were set on race would be conservative.

Joan wore sweaters and, at that time, what they called pedal pushers, now referred to as capris. Tight at the bottom and cinched at the hips, they highlighted her full rich inviting figure. The sweaters she wore draped her breasts and gave them a delicious movement even when she was just sitting and turning her head. Proportionately, this was the most perfect woman I had ever seen all in one package. Not a feast for the eyes, but a banquet. Her sweaters showed no bra line, so my imagination ran wild with the thought of those bare breasts with so little to restrain them. So close at times I need only to accidentally lean and brush next to her to feel the warmth and softness of them. This I did only one time during an activity in which she was close to me. When it occurred it felt like I had put my finger in a wall socket, the current racing from head to toe winding up in my groin and urging it to awake.

On this particular day of the contact, she gave me a quizzical look and I responded with, "Oh, I'm sorry. It was an accident." (Me thinketh I protesteth too much.)

"That's all right, no harm done. Listen, I've been meaning to ask you about cutting my lawn. As you know, I don't have any kids and I'm getting tired of doing it alone. Frank is always working and doesn't have the time."

I, not thinking of this as anything but another lawn to do, responded negatively, "Well, I've got quite a few on my list now, maybe I can find you someone else, OK?"

"No," she quickly snapped, "I want you."

Boing! What did she say? "OK," I heard myself say. "I'll come down after school tomorrow and see what it's going to take."

She softened immediately, seeing she was going to get her way (what she was used to). "Great, that will be swell. I'll fix you a treat. You'll probably want a snack or something by that time of day."

(Oh, I wanted a snack or something okay.) "See you tomorrow, Mrs. Martin."

"Call me Joan, will you? Mrs. Martin makes me feel old."

"All right, Joan." (She was pushing thirty hard, but no more…old?)

The next day at school, my mind was so full of Mrs. Martin I left my books outside at lunch, forgot my locker combination, and got on the wrong bus to go home.

Rushing into the room I shared with my brother, Barry (two years younger), I remembered it was his day to cut our lawn. We alternated each week. Usually, I took him along on my mowing jobs and shared the money with him. Things have a way of working out sometimes. I told mom I was going over to do Mrs. Martin's lawn and might be late for supper. She gave this announcement no great concern and later I learned Joan had asked her if it was OK. As Joan had her own lawn-mower and equipment (some equipment), I had time to clean up some-what and rush out the back door, cutting through the neighbor's yard 'til I reached the Martin's house. I was tingling with expectancy.

Mrs. Martin's house wasn't what I expected…decorated in Ethan Allen colonial period furniture that I felt was more his taste than hers. She met me at the door as quickly as I rang the bell. She wore shorts and a very thin sweater that left no doubt she wasn't wearing anything else.

"Hi, Bobby, come on in. I have a treat for you," she purred.

Joan was unusual in that she wore little or no makeup. Her skin glis-tened with a freshness that gave her a glow. Her lipstick, if any, appeared to be natural, adding a softness and shape men ache to kiss.

The little kitchen nook was set up with blue (my favorite color) accessories and a plate of sandwiches and fresh potato salad.

While serving me, she caught me looking at her breasts and smiled, "I think you are a lot older for your age than most people realize."

I squirmed and didn't know quite what to say when she offered, "Listen, I asked you to come over to do my lawn, but I also wanted to talk to you. I've noticed you don't have much to do with the girls your age, why not?"

I don't know why, but I told her all of it…my fears, dreams and sex-ual escapades. At first she seemed shocked, then excited. "Isn't it nice to have someone to talk to about this? I felt you needed a good friend and if you want, I'll be that friend. Whatever we tell each other stays our secret, OK?"

I wasn't perceiving anything, just that she seemed to care. We finished our snack and she told me she would walk around the lawn and show me what she wanted done.

While she pointed out the type of upkeep she wanted, I found myself getting lost in her looks again. She walked as if never lifting her feet, but effectively gliding the distance she needed to travel. I've seen this in very few women and was never disappointed, as this grace normally meant great coordination, strength and fine sexual prowess. Joan went on about the trimming as I kept marveling at her movement.

Suddenly she snapped, "Bobby, you're not listening to a thing I'm telling you, are you?"

Luckily, I remembered just enough of what she had said to convince her I had listened.

"Well, I would like for you to cut back that corner bush now. It's driving me crazy rubbing against my bedroom window when the wind blows.

I agreed and went to the tool shed to get what I needed. I daydreamed as I worked and cut back more of the bush than I should have. She had gone in and cleaned up the kitchen and returned to help me bag up the clippings. "Whew, we've both worked up a sweat. Let's get something cold to drink, OK?"

Following her into the house, I found my eyes riveted on her tight bottom to the extent that I was becoming aroused.

She had turned on the air so the coolness enveloped us as we walked in.

"How about some of my special lemonade?"

"What makes it special?" I asked, trying to sit down right away so the obvious wouldn't be.

"You'll see," she laughingly shot back. "By the way, did you tell your mother you would be late?"

"Yes, she knows."

"Well, I also told her I had a few things I needed help with so you might be later than usual."

I let this statement sink in as the special lemonade arrived. She had apparently fixed a pitcher full while I was outside. I queried, "Tell me about Frank. I really haven't had a chance to talk to him much."

"Frank's a wonderful person. We've been married for over five years and get along beautifully. He's a numismatic, that's a coin collector. It takes up most of his spare time when he's not working. He was an only child and so, like me, doesn't see the need for us to have children. In fact, we have separate bedrooms."

At this bit of information, I paid closer attention, "Do you mean you don't sleep together?" I daringly asked.

"Oh, we get together occasionally, but that's not his thing."

I have always been amazed at the secrets seemingly normal people have. "Doesn't that bother you?"

"Well, it took some getting used to, but he's good to me in so many other ways it works. Listen, you've sweated through those clothes you're in. Why don't you go in the bedroom and hand them out the door to me. I can throw them in the wash and dry in no time."

I didn't even give it a second thought. Like a trained puppy, I drained my second glass of her special lemonade, which seemed to get better and better. Once in the bedroom, I stripped and was so glad my mother always insisted on clean and neat underwear. I cracked the door and handed them to her. She suddenly pushed the door open further saying, "Oh, I forgot to tell you, there's a nice shower back there. Why don't you wash up while I'm doing these and I'll get you another lemonade."

Her eyes had traveled my entire length while she was talking to me and ended with a deep look into my eyes as if to say, "That will do."

I had just gotten past that breathless experience of those hot stinging pellets of water embedding the heat in my body when the shower door opened and closed quickly. I felt her close to me, "Here's your lemonade."

I could barely see through the steam and felt for the glass more than saw it. Her hands soaped me, massaging investigatingly, getting where no one had before. She did it slowly and I rose to the occasion and gulped down my lemonade...

She opened the shower door and took the glass and placed it on the bedside stand. To do this, she had to walk, dripping wet, across the carpet. The Venetian blinds and curtains were drawn, but burning rays of light lit up the symphony of suppleness her body displayed.

As she turned to return to the shower, she grabbed a small pouch from the bed. She held it hidden in her hand. This made me apprehensive, which she noticed and cooed, "Now, now, I'm not going to do anything you won't like."

"But, what about your husband?"

"Oh, he's going to Birmingham after work to buy a set of coins. He won't be back until very late."

She kissed me tenderly, gently and longingly...slowly showing me how she liked to be kissed. She liked to be kissed and nibbling her lips, I felt I had never really kissed another until now. I left the lusciousness of her mouth and traveled down to finally get a mouthful of those beautifully firm breasts with nipples that I had only seen in magazines. (I remembered Joan years later when I saw a playboy layout of Anita Ekberg.)

Our playful foreplay finally ended in a toweling that finished on the big king sized bed's silk pillows, piled high and matching the silk sheets. Lying on the silk was enough to drive me crazy.

Joan moved me into the positions she liked, slowly, with little pressures of her hands and inquiring movements of her head. She purred like a cat. At first, I thought I was imagining the low, throaty, soft rumblings from her throat. She suddenly rolled me over on my back by crossing my feet and turning them like a steering wheel, a trick I never forgot.

The mysterious thing in her left hand finally appeared and I felt her manipulate my bottom and slip something into me. I was apprehensive but not scared as she rolled me back over and mounted me. She rose to each climax slowly, rhythmically, hypnotizing me with the rocking movement of her hips. Her burning lips just brushing mine occasionally. She placed my hands on her breasts, pinching my fingers to her nipples until I had the exact pressure on them she wanted. She whispered to me, "Why don't you let go?"

I replied, "I want to satisfy you first."

"You mean you can keep this up?"

"Even more than this," I proudly announced.

"Show me," she challenged.

I threw my legs over the side of the bed with her still on top. I pulled her legs around me until she was sitting on my lap with that beautiful bare bottom in my hands between my legs. I pulled her closer to me and pounded myself deeper and deeper into her, stretching those muscles rarely used until you do a lot of splits.

Watching a woman's face as you bring her pleasure is one of the most beautiful things a man can behold. Moments of surprise, gentle smiles of rapture, incredible gasps of delight…these are just a few if you are reading her body right.

Joan's stamina was incredible, her recovery almost instant as one climax flowed into another. I rolled her over on her back and made her close her legs with me still inside her, slowly bending into the upper part as I went into the downward strokes. The muscles of her thighs were rigid, her hips moving as if she was on a bicycle. She leaned up again and softly, breathlessly, asked me to finish.

I've always had the ability to hold as long as I wanted to and then relax and let myself get lost in the moment. I think you are born with this, it isn't something you learn.

As I let myself get lost in her, I felt her hand reaching behind me searching for something. As I reached the top of that molten mountain, I stopped suddenly as she pulled a knot of the cord out of me. My passion rose again, released and just as the fall commenced, she pulled another knot and I began again. I can't tell you how many times that occurred, only that I had never released that many times and in that volume and that hard. My jaw muscles locked up and knots of stomach muscles belted my middle. The air left me and I breathed in gulps, hyperventilating until I passed out.

I woke to her hand and a washcloth of cool water soothing my body, "You're something else, Bobby. How long have you been sexually active?"

"One way or another, all my life. Why?"

"I doubt other people would ever suspect what you are capable of."

"You mean I satisfied you?"

"You gave me a hunger for more, something I had not planned on."

Joan showered with me and helped me get dressed in the clothes warm from the dryer. She caressed me as I slipped them on, and I felt I had just fulfilled that young fantasy that all puberty age males have. I kept thinking that someone was going to wake me any minute.

"Joan, I." She put her hand over my mouth and said quickly, "Don't say a word. Both of us enjoyed the moment and hopefully, we'll have many more. Now give me a kiss and get that sweet body of yours home. I'll call you and we'll set up the day for you to do the lawn."

Arriving home, I was paranoid some family member would notice the rosy glow and my beaming demeanor. The closest anyone came was my oldest sister when she leaned over and observed I sure smelled awfully good to have been cutting lawns all afternoon. Luckily, this went unheard by mother, but dad did give me an inquiring look.

Mondays were Joan's days and I went straight over there from school. She always met me at the door with her special lemonade and a snack prepared. Those days were filled with wonderful hours of new exciting adventures. She was inventive and taught me to explore. She dressed up for me and taught me to role-play. She posed for Polaroids and reveled in the posing, but she would burn all the pictures after each session. I was always apprehensive about Frank coming home during one of those sessions and worried what he would do.

It wasn't Frank that discovered us this particular day. I had just finished the lawn and was talking to Joan through the shower door as she lay on the bed when the doorbell rang. This didn't concern me too much as it had happened before. Joan would take care of it by telling the visitor that she didn't feel well and was lying down.

As I toweled off, she gave me the hush sign and slipped on a silky robe. As the bedroom was in the back of the house, I couldn't hear the conversation. I heard voices move into the living room, which meant she had invited them in. I sneaked into the front bedroom to see if I could identify the vehicle they came in.

The 1956 blue and white station wagon was hard to miss! I froze. It was my family's car! But who was out there? Usually dad drove the car, although sometimes mother drove him to work so she could shop. (It was unusual, in those days, for a family to have two cars.) Think! Think! Did mom drive him to work? As the school bus left early, I didn't know either way. That feeling of insects crawling up my back overtook me as fear showed itself physically.

The voices from the living room continued to drone and sweat popped out on my brow. I waited, holding my breath until becoming aware of this situation by gasping for air. I could feel and hear my heart. Finally, after what seemed like hours, I heard the door open and close and I heard the car start up and drive away.

Joan called me and I came out of hiding. She informed me it had been my mother who came over to pick me up if I was finished. As we lived only two streets away, I suspected it was more than that, "What did you tell her?"

Joan laughed, "Calm down, I told her we had just made love and you were showering."

"What? Are you crazy?"

Joan laughed even harder and with that playful glint in her eyes said, "I told her you were down the street borrowing some gas, as we had run out and that you wouldn't be done for a while. Your mother said that would be okay and she would keep your supper warm."

Relief was just a swallow away as I breathed deeply again. "Joan, you shouldn't joke like that, you almost gave me a heart attack."

Joan laughed again, "Well, if there's one thing that will never fail you it's your heart. It's strong and will get you through all you'll need. Now come here and let me make you feel better." (Boing!)

*   *   *

I remember it was raining that day. I hated it when it rained on Monday, as I had little or no excuse to go over to Joan's. I was in my room sulking when I heard the phone ring and heard mother say, "Oh, hi Joan. Yes, he's here. Do you want me to get him? Oh, all right, I'm sure he'll be glad to."

I raced down the hall too quickly and caught myself just as she gave me a startled look. "Well, I wish you came that fast when I call you, anyway, Joan wants you to come over for a few minutes and lift something down from the attic in the garage, OK?"

"Sure, mom, I'll hurry so I won't be late for dinner."

"Oh, she said it would take only a few minutes and she'd have you back in no time."

Heading over to Joan's house, I pondered that remark (A few minutes?). What was she thinking? Something was wrong.

When I arrived at the house, Joan opened the door immediately and the look on her face was one I hadn't seen before. It was that 'I have something I don't want to tell you' look. She made small talk about what a wonderful relationship we had and how she looked forward to seeing me each week. I sensed the ending before she told me. Frank was being transferred and they would be moving in two weeks.

My world collapsed. This was the sunshine in my life, something I looked forward to as I got up each day. What was I going to do? Joan reached out and held me understanding my bewilderment. "Nothing is forever," she whispered, "so you make each day as special as you can, because eventually they become few and far between."

I left the house and cried all the way home, knowing that the rain would hide the wetness, though I didn't really care. I always thought it was a game, sex and companionship, and now realized I had fallen in love with her and needed her as a person in my life, not just a sexual fantasy.

I saw her only one more time when she and Frank had dinner at our house before they left. Oh, I had made many excuses to go over to her house, but I later figured out she must have been home a number of times, but she didn't answer the door. I fantasized she had fallen in love with me and didn't want to hurt me with another goodbye. I was surprised the day my mother gave me a key to Joan's house, which was up for sale, and said Joan called and wanted me to check if she turned off her water heater.

I went to her house and upon entering, recalled the experiences we had enjoyed. Funny how the little things stick in your mind, like the Carolina blue plates she served snacks on. I could still visualize them in the breakfast nook…the shower door with the softly opaque etch that let you see just enough to titillate…even the rich Kelly green carpet in the bedroom. I took my shoes and socks off just to feel and remember the times we wound up there and the burns it left on my knees.

I had done a lot of odds and ends around the house, one of which was to fix a bad water heater connection, so I knew where it was and checked it out. Taped to the control box was a note. I recognized Joan's handwriting as she had left me notes when she was going to be late. They would make me laugh, like "I can hardly wait, don't start without me!"

The note simply said to check the drop. The drop was a bottle behind the certain bush we both used to communicate if something went wrong.

I found the bottle and in it a note that said, "Buy something you've always wanted and couldn't have and think of me, Love, Joan."

Inside were ten one hundred dollar bills. I was stunned. This was more money than I had ever seen and it was all mine! Then I felt bad, thinking I should send it back to her, but how? If it fell into the wrong hands, it would cause a lot of trouble. I put the money back in the bottle and started to hide it again but worried that someone might find it before she came back. (They had to come back for closing.)

I put the money in my pocket. Tears filled my eyes as I walked home thinking what a wonderful thing she had done. I always wondered if she was just using me. The money seemed to be her way of saying, "Even though I'm not with you, I still love you and want you to be happy."

I bought my first car with that money. I told my parents I had saved the money from cutting lawns. Barry was suspicious, so I gave him a hundred dollars and he was happy. I bought small presents for my sisters so they wouldn't feel left out. I never saw Joan again but remembered her every time I drove.

Chapter 7

RACHEL

My family returned again to the U.S. where my father was stationed in El Paso, Texas, then Aberdeen, Maryland, and wound up in Huntsville, Alabama. I didn't learn until later that my father was quite smart, working his way up through the ranks and attending Officer's Candidate School in Fort Benning, Georgia. (One of the oldest sergeants to do so.) After serving in the 101st and 82nd Air Borne Divisions, he had achieved expert ratings on every hand weapon the army had, signified on his uniform by a full ladder of medals. He had medals from World War II and the Korean War and apparently was well thought of by his superiors.

We came to Huntsville so my father could work with Wernher Von Braun's team of missile experts. (They designed the Nike missile programs.) My father, now in ordinance, helped design the field application of the weapon so even a foot soldier with limited education could set it up, aim, and fire it with ease.

Huntsville, Alabama, at first glance, was a typical southern city. The center was the square with a courthouse in the middle, with statues of Confederate and World War II veterans out front. The square was surround by the usual assortment of shops, cafes and hardware stores.

Redstone Arsenal was an Ordinance Depot built and manned pre-World War II to develop weapons for the U.S. Army. Suddenly, the cold war exploded and the race for space developed. Hence, Marshall Space Flight Center was created and NASA sprang to life. The small city was besieged by scientists and their families looking for housing. Most lived up on Monte Santo Mountain where army security could keep an eye on them. The German group, led by Wernher Von Braun (father of the U.S. missile program), had grand estates with tight security. My father had to attend parties at his house (called command performances) by order. He never said much about those visits, but mother went along and shared some of the aesthetics of the estates.

We moved into a ranch-style, three-bedroom home at 2217 Tanglewood Circle. It was located off Governor's Drive across from A&M College, at that time all black. The drive to work took dad only half an hour; so most times he was home by 6:00 p.m. Dinner had to be on the table and we, the two sons and two daughters, had to be cleaned up and seated and ready to eat. Mom was a great cook and even during the years we lived on enlisted pay and had very little, she always came up with a meal we relished. I remember we lived in a converted mule barn one time in Fort Benning, Georgia, and when we had meat once a week in spaghetti sauce, we considered it quite a treat.

Huntsville meant high school and more pain. I was unaccepted by the other kids because of my demeanor and dating practices. (Different because of the transition from European girls to American girls.) My brothers and sisters were not readily accepted. My sister, Judy, did better…blonde, blue-eyed and with the stature of Twiggy, she won most people over and made friends. I, however, became the person always referred to as, "What's his name?"

The abuse from my father continued, so I was looking for any way to leave home permanently. When graduation time came at the old Huntsville High School, I was not allowed to participate. They called me in and told me some courses I had taken at Kaiserlauten High School in Germany weren't recognized. I would have to go another year to get my diploma.

This news, to say the least, was devastating. Another year here? No way!

The University of Maryland had an extension campus in Huntsville at that time because of the Marshall Space Flight Center and NASA. I took their offered GED course test and passed with flying colors. Getting my diploma that way hurt. Later on, I took some other courses to earn some college credits through the mail.

Diploma in hand, I went down and enlisted in a special program the Navy offered called the Polaris Sub Program. I had scored high on my pre-testing and was qualified to enlist under this, but not guaranteed service in the subs, just an opportunity.

After boot camp, I found myself designated to attend radar school instead. I served four years and was fairly happy and used to the discipline, as I had grown up with it.

The loss of my father and little sister, Charlene, in an automobile accident in Bedford, Virginia, brought me home on emergency leave to Huntsville.

My father was dead and I remember the rage I felt not being able to tell him things I had always wanted to. The funeral, full military and well attended, was a blur. I escorted mother to the car as the grave service ended. God apparently decided he had rained on me long enough. A veil lifted and an angel appeared, this time for real, in the form (and I do mean form) of a stunning redhead with heart-stopping green eyes. I sat with the car door open. She approached and the sun behind her made a halo effect with her curls, "I want to express my sympathy," she said softly. "My name is Rachel."

When you meet someone under those circumstances, you naturally don't expect to see them again. This was not to be the case. Mother, who had been driving the car at the time of the accident, was still trying to ease the discomfort of her arm in a cast. "Oh, I wish I could feel normal again!"

"Mom, you have to get on with your life. Let me take you to the beauty shop to get fixed up and I'll take you out to dinner."

She refused at first, but then I reminded her that I had only two weeks left before I had to report back to base. She consented to the salon, but said she would think about dinner.

Mom made an appointment for the next day and informed that the woman who did her hair was Rachel's mother. Strange how things come together in life.

I asked about Rachel and mom told me she had a baby boy whose father had decided to run off rather than face the responsibility.

Driving mom to the salon, a very small corner building in the lower-income section of Huntsville, I wondered if Rachel would be there. I still remembered that angelic moment when she appeared out of the sun.

The shop had only two stations—a sink and one hair dryer. Mrs. Robinson, Rachel's mother, was the owner-operator. She met us with a big "Hello," stopping her curler efforts with her client and giving mother a big hug. "Charlotte, it's so good to see you out and about. It's the best thing for you. This must be your oldest you are always talking about. My he's handsome."

Mrs. Robinson took mother under her wing and sat me down with magazines. I finally found a 'Look' after flipping through four or five 'Better Homes and Gardens' and 'Hair Styles by so and so.'

Suddenly, the door opened and there she was, damp ringlets outlining her face and glistening perspiration glistening at her throat, "Well, it's a hot one out there today. I had to take Robbie to the sitter and she had only one fan working in the house, so I went home and got out the extra one so she and the baby would stay cool."

I was still in my whites as I hadn't brought any civilian clothes with me…bell bottoms, single zipper front pants with the over-the-head V-front square back shirt the Navy was known for. My black kerchief, rolled and tied in what appeared to be a square knot, was done with a fake slider. My black "Boone Dockers" were spit-shined to a mirror glaze (my inspection pair), even with the little attention for the last couple of days, reflected all thrown their way.

I stood up as she entered, now at six feet tall, my frame still slight at 169 pounds. "Hi, thank you for coming to the funeral. We really appreciated it."

For the first time, those green eyes locked into my blue ones digging deep. "I really liked your father. He dropped your mother off here many times. Sometimes he came early to pick her up and we talked and got to know one another."

As she talked, I was fascinated by her mouth. Her bottom lip seemed to be in a petulant pout, yet along with her throaty voice able to dictate a tenseness unlike any I had experienced before.

She went on to say other nice things about my mother, but my mind drifted. My eyes were busy, blessed by the lush curves, promising hips and deep milk-heavy breasts damp through the short, thin, beige cotton dress, the button front straining from the extra weight of her recent pregnancy.

"How old is your baby?" I blurted out, not knowing why.

"He's two months old." She produced a hospital picture taken at his birth. A small image of red rawness not representing his mother's beauty, but bright red hair matching hers. "His name is Robbie."

I nervously slipped a cigarette out of my pack and offered her one. "We can't smoke in here. Would you like to step outside and have one with me?" I offered.

"No, I have to help mother with her other appointments. Maybe later." And she was a blur, sweeping up, cleaning the stations and waiting on customers. Every now and then, she threw a puzzled look at me.

Mother had decided to get a permanent and the smell of which, in spite of my desire to watch Rachel, drove me outside for a smoke.

Huntsville in the summer is a humid horror, a wet heat that drives itself deep into your pores until they weep for relief. Within minutes, I had soaked through my uniform and had to take off my lid (white hat) to wipe the excess sweat from its band.

The rush of the cool interior air blessed me as the door of the beauty shop opened and Rachel slipped out. "I can't believe you've been out there so long, it's so hot."

"I'm used to it. We put up with worse aboard ship sometimes."

"Do you have a filter tip?"

"No, I smoke Pall-Malls. Sorry, but you're welcome to one."

"OK, I'll try one, but they're probably too strong."

I lit one for her and carefully handed it to her.

"That's so sexy, I've never had anyone light my cigarette that way."

"Sorry, I wasn't thinking. I feel I've known you before."

"You know, I feel the same way, it's spooky."

I moved a locket of hair from her eyes and she tensed up immediately. "Don't do that please."

"I'm sorry," I replied instantly. "I just think your eyes are beautiful and wanted to see them better."

Losing my father and little sister, Charlene, had stripped my emotions bare, leaving a loss of control I hadn't realized until now.

"Listen, I didn't mean anything. I'm just wiped out by the funeral and all. Please don't take that wrong."

Suddenly, she hugged me with tears running down her lovely cheeks. I stiffened and after the shock, returned the hug. We stood there in silence for what seemed an eternity (actually a few minutes). She pushed away and apologized, "I'm sorry, we've both been through a lot lately. It's just nice to feel close to someone. I have to go in."

She tossed the little-used cigarette down and stomped on it as if mad at herself for the emotion she had shown and went back in without another word.

Entering the shop again, I realized our silhouettes had been outlined through the frosted glass and the ladies were trying to act as if they hadn't seen anything. My mother gave me a look as if to say, "I'll talk to you later." I crept over to the corner of the shop and picked up a 'Vanity Fair', and acted as if I was thoroughly engrossed in it…but stealing glances, trying to figure out where Rachel had gone.

She appeared out of the back bathroom with tear-stained eyes, red and swollen. "Mrs. Richardson, let's get these curlers out and see what we've got here." She refused to glance my way as if afraid she would lose it again. I tried to maintain an outward appearance of disinterest, but was boiling inside remembering the wonderful softness of her body against mine.

Mother was through, so we said our "Goodbyes" and drove home.

"What was that all about outside the shop?" she asked.

My silence was met by a concerned stare. "Bobby, look, you've been on an emotional roller coaster these past few weeks and still are on one. Walk slowly and get your breath or you will make bad decisions, OK?"

"OK, mom."

A few days went by and I became bored with the doing nothing routine of suburbia. Mother returned to working as a nurse at Huntsville Hospital at my urging. With her gone, the house was empty and full of painful memories. I found the phone number of the beauty shop. While dialing, I was thinking it would be nice just to talk to her.

Her mother answered the phone and informed me that Rachel was at home. Her sitter had an emergency and couldn't keep the baby.

I asked for her home number and her mother, after a lengthy pause, gave it to me.

Rachel answered the phone as if she was expecting it to ring. I could hear the disappointment in her voice when she realized it wasn't whom she thought (the baby's father).

"Hey, I just thought I'd call and see if you wanted to go to the drive-in tonight."

"Oh, Bob, that would be nice but I can't. My sitter is tied up and mom has to go somewhere. I don't have anyone to care for Robbie."

"Bring him along," I heard myself say.

"Really…you wouldn't mind? It's been so long since I've gone any-where. It would be great."

"Rachel, look, right now we both need to escape, have some fun and relax. I'll pick you up at six so we can stop at the Oasis and get a snack before the movie. (Oasis was a drive-thru carhop hangout.)

"That's great, we'll split the bill. I work you know."

"No this is my treat. I have to leave soon."

"OK, see you at six," and she hung up.

I mentally danced for about half an hour 'till I realized I had no idea where she lived. I called the house but there was no answer. (I found out later she had gone to the shop to get fixed up.) I thought about calling the shop for directions, but after the pause her mother had given me, I didn't want to combat that. I looked up her name in the phone book and found the address. I learned long ago that the local fire station could give you better directions than anyone. So, after another phone call, I was set.

Rachel was all of eighteen years old (the first woman younger than me). She had grown up in Huntsville, Alabama. I knew little about her father except that he had run off and left her mother with a son just walking and Rachel, a newborn. (History repeats itself.)

She grew up quickly, first working out of the house doing hair, and then finally getting her beautician's license.

Her brother, Richard, was a race car enthusiast. In those days, stock car racing didn't make money. He constantly brought home old cars, parked them in the yard and worked on them intermittently…hope-fully to sell.

Rachel was a real beauty. She had entered a couple of local beauty contests and won. Being left with a baby after her first love was not as accepted in those days (single mother and all) as it is today.

Rachel, without makeup, had a raw beauty. Flaming hair and white-washed skin gave her an older look. One would think she was a "seen the world" type, when actually she had seen and done so little.

She stood five-seven with hips that helped anything that hung on them look good, ample breasts, and shoulders that looked like they didn't need shoulder pads to outline the oval face and petulant (I want my own way) lips.

With cosmetics, she could pass for a movie star, and on a man's arm drew glances of interest and admiration.

Needless to say, I was a goner…

That evening at the drive-in proved to both of us we were moving too quickly. After putting the baby to sleep in the back seat, we petted and explored each other like two kids enjoying the journey, but knowing that this was just the beginning.

I drove home with both of us frustrated but still glowing with youthful desire. "Thank you so much for taking me and Robbie out like this. I really think you're neat for doing it." She reached over and kissed me deep and laughingly. "Hope to see you soon."

I handed the baby over, who was sleeping as if in a coma. She cuddled him close, looking at him with that mother-love look. The smell of fresh baby powder filled my nostrils as I leaned closer to catch a last glimpse of the little feller.

The next day, I called Rachel and asked if she could get away for the evening as I thought we would drive to Birmingham and have dinner there. She was so exited, "Birmingham! How did you know I wanted to go to Birmingham? Let me call you back. I have to see if mother can watch Robbie for me."

Rachel called back to say she could and would go.

I pulled up in a borrowed convertible a friend lent me. He lived next door and I used to wash and wax it for him so he would let me drive it—a black 1959 409 Chevy Impala that would smack you back in your seat and go through first and second gear before it would let you back up.

Rachel's eyes were rolling when I pulled up. She ran out shouting, "Oh, what a beautiful car, is it yours? Did you buy it? Are we taking this to Birmingham?" not stopping for a breath.

"No, I borrowed it and yes, we are taking it to Birmingham." I loaded a little cosmetics box and overnight bag quickly into the trunk without pointing out the obvious. She intended to spend the night with me.

The trip to Birmingham was like a movie. We pretended to be a wealthy couple who were traveling just to pass the time…stopping by all the tourist sights and Confederate War markers as if we were documenting a long trip. She had brought a Brownie and went to great pains to take pictures set up a certain way and had others take our picture numerous times. I'll admit to this day, I've never seen any of those and always wanted to.

Birmingham was a major industrial city, one of the oldest and largest in Alabama. Downtown had the dirt, but was known for its factory row houses with their freshly scrubbed stoops (front steps to those of you ignorant of city jargon).

I had been to Birmingham but once before, then only on a bus to somewhere else. So we both reveled in the search for a place to spend the night. I had a little money now, as my past checks had come, so I decided on a hotel, not a motel.

I can't remember the name of the place, but I will not forget the front entrance. In its days, it must have been one of the grand hotels. The canopy out front, hanging by golden bronze rods, was coupled into a latticework of intricate patterns of swirls and leaves edging the canopy as if holding it together. The gold in the bronze had a greenish hue from the heavy humidity in the air. The white marble portico pillars leading up to the entrance were veined by green and black, giving it almost a cracked look. The "whoosh-whoosh" of the circular door as it revolved allowing one to enter, reminded me of the hotels of New York and Rockefeller Center.

The shiny brass revolving door was a mystery to Rachel, so I hopped along side her and showed her how to push through and emerge into the lobby where time had stood still.

Age had taken its toll. The once red and black oriental carpeting was a bit gray in places and had the smell of disinfectant from too many cleanings. The circular pillars in the middle seating stations, just off the main desk and elevators, needed only black satin show shams to give it back to the Victorian era it was designed for. The bellman (boy would have been a real stretch) struggled to handle the small cosmetic case and overnight bag from Rachel, allowing me to carry my Samsonite without objections.

The desk was manned by a matronly woman with the "We run a respectable hotel" look written all over her face.

I boldly attacked the problem with an opening gambit, "I don't know, dear. This place isn't quite what we had in mind in New York, but it appears to be clean. Shall we find out what is available?"

She gave me that "who the hell do you think you are?" look and said, "We have very few rooms available as we are currently renovating…almost half the hotel. However, there are rooms and they are quite nice."

I shoved two one hundred dollar bills toward her and said, "That will be fine, ma'am. I'm looking forward to seeing this grand hotel returned to its original opulence."

I signed in as Mr. and Mrs. and reached for the key.

Rachel nervously blurted out, "This is the most beautiful hotel I have ever seen!"

The desk woman gave me that, "I knew it all along" look and told the bellman, "Room 201."

The elevator, an old-fashioned one, still had to be operated manually. The bellman, obviously not used to it, took two tries to line us up on the second floor.

Surprisingly, the room was not what I expected. Double entry doors entered into a suite. The master bedroom was on the left and to the right a massive living room with a bar and fireplace. The room was done in gold with woven brocade wallpaper, heavy oak chair rail and cornices. The furniture, overstuffed and fading from age, still was clean and the smell of age, although apparent, overridden by a potpourri pleasing to the senses.

Seeing someone you've fallen for naked for the first time should be done slowly, so that a mental brush can softly paint the pallet of memories with the soft rich textures of the moment.

Watching Rachel undress was mesmerizing. She enjoyed the moment, letting each garment linger down her body to the floor. The lighting was just right, as the old yellowed cloth shades of the standing brass lamps lit up her skin with a glow. Her hair flamed over every movement as though her body was on fire. The nipples of her heavy breasts were diving through the strands of curls in and out as she moved.

I had not seen how beautiful her back was. The arch just above her pelvic bone looked as if Michelangelo had carved it just for me. As she moved with the mystery of a cat about to do something you can't quite figure out, I motioned for her to turn around. She did me one better, pirouetting again and again.

Those toned buttocks and rhythmically motored hips reached out and hugged my mind. Her womanhood appeared surprisingly bare until I noticed the hair around it was almost white blond and light red, almost pink in the light available.

In spite of her recent pregnancy, her ribs were still sculptured and framed her chest majestically.

To my surprise, she showed no false modesty, but reveled in my eyes molesting her every movement. We said nothing, knowing that it was not necessary. I, too, had been disrobing and she made a pleasing noise when I finally exposed my manhood. Then she smiled, reaching for me and leading me to the bedroom where she had already rolled the covers back and had the stage set for our sexual passage.

For the next two days we lived in that room. We called Rachel's' mother to explain we needed another day to see everything and giggled at the double meaning. That probably was the happiest we had both been in our lives.

We were free from all restraints and absolutely unaware of the world around us. I managed a candlelight supper in our room surreptitiously. Rachel cried like a baby when I told her to get dressed and why. She said she had only read about things like that and dreamed of someday doing them.

The simple things are more valuable in memory than anything material or complicated.

After arriving back in Huntsville after acting like newlyweds on the way home, we had agreed to tell both our mothers at once that, yes, we were engaged and I was going to adopt Robbie as my own.

Needless to say, her mother was overjoyed and mine was beside herself.

The original plan was for Rachel to stay in Huntsville, either at her mother's or mine, until I got out of the Navy. Then we could do what we wanted. (The best laid plans of mice and women.)

Rachel became increasingly upset as the day of my departure back to the west coast drew closer. She threw tantrums, insisting that if I loved her so much, how could I go off and leave her and the baby.

I countered with the facts of income, no relatives for her to lean on, all alone on the west coast when I went to sea for weeks and months, all to no avail. She was determined to come with me. Finally, it became an ultimatum. Love is blind, lust creates stupidity. The combination deadens out the brain and movement to the nearest cliff.

I left Huntsville after being married at the courthouse downtown and a one-night honeymoon at the 'Heart of Huntsville Hotel'. My new family flew to San Francisco to meet my ship.

I rented a two room flat in Oakland, across the bay from San Francisco, stocked it with groceries, kissed the baby and Rachel goodbye and reported for duty.

She had no phone, little money and almost no way of reaching me or I her. I couldn't tell her how long it would be before I got my first liberty, so we both realized what a horrible situation we were in.

Reporting to my ship the USS Currituck AV 7, a seaplane tender, I found out I was scheduled for liberty in two days. Those were the longest and loneliest in memory, not knowing if they were all right. I asked everyone I could if anyone was going near that address in Oakland. No luck. I had intended to pass on a note from me telling when I would be home. No luck.

Finally liberty! Down the gangway I ran hurrying to catch the bus that ran hourly to Oakland. The bus stopped ten blocks from where we rented, so by the time I hit the front door I was not only winded, but scared. I was afraid I didn't have the right place as no one answered the door.

Suddenly, I heard my name and turned and saw my landlady scurrying across the street, "She and the baby are over with me. You shouldn't go off and leave her without saying when you'd' be back...she's been crying for two days and the baby is running a temperature. You should be ashamed of yourself off gallivanting around while your family has barely enough to eat!"

I couldn't believe my ears. Why was this woman so upset with me? Doesn't she realize the Navy sends you where they want, when they want and how they want?

Rachel was a mess...tear-stained swollen face and a thin housecoat with stains down the front. She was standing in the hallway holding Robbie who was crying his heart out. "I didn't think you were coming back for us. I thought you had changed your mind and were just going to let us go back to Huntsville."

"Rachel, you are my wife and I love you very much, but you are going to have to realize the situation we are in and try to make the best of it. This has been only two days. If we had ship's movement (when a vessel is ordered to stand to and serve elsewhere), it could have been two months! Now I have only 72 hours to get you set up and ready for my not being here. Let's go home."

Arriving back at our two-room hole-in-the-wall, I couldn't blame her for going stir crazy. The apartment was actually half of a full-sized house. The entrance went into a living room-bedroom combination and into a kitchen with the bath off to the right.

The entrance door was half glass and, with the one kitchen window, allowed little sunlight. The dusty interior was daubed in California umber colors of different shades.

The bed was in a two-door closet on the left wall and pulled down with the headboard attached. The one chair, rusty color and worn, just fit along the other wall with a table and two chairs when the bed was down.

The kitchen ran left to right on the wall directly ahead with an old dome-top Frigidaire, yellowed with age, gasping in the corner. Wall sockets were at a premium as were lights.

Rachel placed the baby in a bassinet I hadn't seen before, set up on the archway into the kitchen and pulled some drapes in front. The baby quit crying and seemed to be going to sleep. I later found out she had rubbed his gums with Paregoric supplied by the landlady.

Rachel pulled down the bed and said, "You haven't even kissed me yet, didn't you miss me?"

I think I knew as I grabbed her and kissed and held her, she would never adjust to this way of life.

She attacked me like an animal. Suddenly and violently she stripped off my uniform, ripping my socks in the process and threw my shoes across the room. (I found them later in the sink.)

Her mouth was all over me. Her eyes had a wild intensity I hadn't seen before, as if she was in a trance. She moaned as we made love physically, she on top pounding me into her and returning the down stroke as if to beat me into submission. Pulling me up, she sat me on the side of the bed, mounted me, and with her legs behind me moved me into her. Her hips were traveling from my knees to my hips, thrusting, thrusting until we were both gasping for air.

I suddenly felt pain on my back. She had slit open the skin with her nails, like a boson doing his job with a cat-o-nine tails. Blood ran down onto the sheets and I noticed my white uniform blouse hadn't quite made it off the bed and was spotted by the liquid intensity of our lovemaking.

Rachel was spent and curled up on the bed. I pulled her into my arms and rocked her to sleep, letting the apparent strain and exhaustion overtake her.

Robbie awoke and needed changing, so I took care of him. I enjoyed his antics. After getting baby powder all over everything, I decided to try to take a bath. He would have none of it, forcing me to disrobe and take him with me.

Playing with the baby in the tub, I wasn't aware of the front door opening and anyone entering. As I got out of the tub with Robbie in hand, I wrapped a giant towel around him. He giggled as I kneaded him dry.

"You're really good with him, you know." It was the landlady. "Here, give him to me and I'll finish while you get dressed. But first, put on your pants, that back needs attention…and don't look so shocked. My old man was Navy and I've rented to military all my life."

I found this reasoning for her ability to invade my privacy didn't make sense, "Don't you knock before you invade someone's privacy?"

Her name was Myrtle and she looked to be in her fifties. Later, I found out she was 63. Her dirty blonde hair combed back in a French roll was held by an ivory comb. Her clothes looked to be sea bag rejects worn thin…a navy button front work shirt, stained Levi bell-bottoms that attacked her ample hips and pinched her waist. Flip-flops and painted toenails set off the outfit.

She flashed her big green eyes my way as she watched me cover my manhood. "I'll run across and get something for your back as soon as I get the baby taken care of. Why don't you take a hot shower and lie down on the bed? I'll be back in a little bit. I think I'll let Robbie sleep over at my place so you two can have a little more privacy." She said the last statement with an emphasis on "a little more."

Rachel stirred and spotted her and with a woman-to-woman look said, "Hi Myrtle, you don't have anything to drink over there do you?"

Myrtle replied, "Sure, come on with me. I'm keeping Robbie tonight so you two can be alone."

While taking a shower (cold), I listened for them to come back. When they didn't, I toweled off, getting blood spots on the towel in the process. My back was a mess and I stretched out on the bed face down. I noticed one of Rachel's fingernails on the sheet. (What was that all about?) I would find out later.

I lay there for what seemed to be a long time waiting for Rachel to return, but succumbed to the softness of the bed and the sexual exhaustion and fell into a deep sleep.

I awoke feeling refreshed. My back didn't hurt and seemed to be tingling. In fact, my whole body seemed to tingle and had a softness like lotion leaves all over. A voice said, "Feel much better now, don't you? Thought I'd never get you rolled over, you were passed out."

I didn't know what to say. It was Myrtle.

"Look, I have two boys of my own and miss them not being around anymore. It was nice making you feel better." She was standing at the end of the bed looking down at me.

I suddenly realized I didn't have a thing on and was aroused. I flipped the sheet over myself and queried her as to where Rachel was.

"Oh, I gave her a Nembutal and a few drinks. She's sleeping it off at my house.

She's probably going to be out for a while. Here, I brought you a drink, I understand you like Jack Daniels.

"Thanks," I muttered as I accepted the glass, hoping a drink would clear my head and I could think. Gulping the drink down, I realized what a dangerous situation I was in and how weak I was with women.

"Myrtle, if you don't mind, I think I'll go over and check on Robbie and bring Rachel back here. We don't have much time. I have to report back tomorrow night for watch."

"I don't think you should wake her up. She has had a very tough two days; a new place, the baby and all, leave well enough alone. Relax! I'm not going to bother you."

(I'm from the IRS, I'm here to help) went though my mind. "OK, but I sure could use another drink." I was thinking she would have to go home to get it.

"Great, I brought the bottle and mix, just in case."

Sitting there talking to Myrtle about Rachel and the baby, I realized Rachel had told her everything. She was aware of my early on willingness to bring them to California and why.

"Tell you what, I have decided to take Rachel and the baby to live with me rent free. I have two bedrooms and all the things that would make them comfortable. I have a phone so you can call when you're away and keep in touch. Before you decide, let me say that at my age, with my husband dead, it gets lonely around here. The neighbors I knew moved away so the company would be great. What do you say?"

I suspected that all of this had been pre-arranged between Rachel and Myrtle later when I noticed most of Rachel's clothes and the baby's were already neatly arranged at Myrtle's (but none of mine). It was plain to see that the two had grown to know each other quickly in those two days I was gone.

Rachel was a different person when I told her it would be okay for her and the baby to stay with Myrtle while I was away, but I insisted on paying part of the rent just to try to establish I had some control of the situation (laugh).

The new few weeks I managed to get home a day or so and found things quite well. Myrtle and Rachel acted like sisters, shared each other's things and the baby was doing fine.

I was scheduled for mid-watch one night and wasn't feeling well and asked the Chief Petty Officer if I could switch with another friend to the port watch. (I was starboard watch and we alternated on nighttime duties when in port.) My friend needed the next night off to visit his relatives coming in. As I left the ship and showed my chit (permission slip) to the Officer of the Deck, I thought what a nice surprise this would be for Rachel.

I stopped on the way home and bought flowers for Rachel and Myrtle and a toy for the baby. As I entered the front door, I heard the shower running and went to the bedroom. Everything was neat and squared away. I found Robbie sleeping peacefully in his bed and removed the bottle from alongside him. A strong smell of Paregoric was present and I spotted a half empty bottle on the bedside stand. Why Paregoric? Was the baby sick again? I wondered. Each bedroom had its own bathroom, so I looked for Rachel in ours and found it empty.

The shower was running in Myrtles' bathroom so I assumed she was taking a shower and Rachel was around somewhere. I looked and found the bedroom door open and the bathroom door ajar. Two silhouettes were outlined through the glass shower door. Through the steam, I watched and listened and learned that Myrtle knew my wife better than I did.

They were enjoying each other too much to know I was there. Sounds I had never heard before nestled in my ears…soft throaty sounds, almost purrs, of delight.

I decided now wasn't the time to confront them. I moved silently toward the front door and swiftly exited the house. I was stunned. What was I to do, ignore this? My stomach was in a knot. I decided, after much pacing, to act like I had not been home yet and enter the house loudly, hoping they would hear me. I re-opened the door and slammed it, "Rachel! Surprise, I'm home!"

I heard frantic movements from Myrtle's bedroom and eventually they both appeared. Rachel had the look of someone caught in the cookie jar and an irritated Myrtle said, "Don't' shout, you'll wake up the baby!" (Fat chance of that.) What are you doing here anyway, are you AWOL?"

"No," I replied, "I switched nights with someone else and thought I'd surprise you."

Rachel ran and gave me a long, lingering kiss. I felt my body tense and fought not to show how upset I was over what I had just witnessed. (I suspected it was more Myrtle's desires than Rachel's.)

Rachel asked, "What's wrong? Are you sick? Your face is so red."

"Yes, I don't feel well, I think I'll go lay down. How's the baby?"

Rachel glanced at Myrtle and said, "He's sleeping a lot better lately so don't bother him."

"OK," I replied and turned to go into the bedroom. It was then I spotted the flowers I had dropped on the carpet outside Myrtle's bedroom along with the baby toy. I ran over and picked them up and presented them to them, hoping they hadn't noticed where the gifts had been. "Here," I offered shakily. "These are for you and this is for the baby."

Myrtle reluctantly accepted hers while giving me a quizzical look and glancing down at the floor where I had picked them up.

I retreated to the bedroom as quickly as I could, undressed and got into bed. Rachel followed me in, undressed and slipped in behind me, pressing her breasts against my back, putting her knees behind mine while kissing the back of my neck. She knew how to push my buttons and she proceeded to push every one. I reluctantly responded at first, then I think the 'I'll show her how good it is to be with a man' thing took over. I went into a trance of sexual athletics that left me breathless and Rachel finally told me she was too sore to continue.

She kissed my cheek and said, "That was the best it's ever been." I felt proud that I had upheld my masculinity, but was still very apprehensive about their relationship. I had to leave in the morning knowing that the woman I loved was sharing the same bed with a lover.

Rachel fell asleep and I got up to get a cigarette. There were none in the room, so I peeked out and spotted a pack next to the couch. Just as I thought I was going to pull this off, Myrtle appeared. Her blonde hair was still moist. She wore a silk Mandarin-style green robe loosely tied over a body I had not really looked at closely before. One side draped open revealing a dark nipple at the tip of an ample breast. Beads of moisture made the silk cling to her skin and patches of translucent dry silk outlined her shape as the light from the window behind her hid all of her face but her big green eyes. She walked toward me like a big cat after its prey. Her voice was husky as she said, "You shouldn't walk around naked like that when I'm around. You forget I'm a widow."

She reached toward me and with relief, I realized she was reaching for a cigarette. I lit hers and then mine.

I started back to my bedroom and she tugged on my arm. "Stay and talk to me a minute, please."

I reluctantly sat down on the couch. She sat down across from me with that physically trim body dancing mental melodies through my psyche. I caught myself staring at her womanhood as she crossed her legs. "Do you find me attractive?"

I was at a loss to respond, hypnotized by the situation I was in.

"I think you do and would like to do something about it."

I remained verbally impotent.

"Rachel and I have discussed this (explosion in my brain) and have decided, as we have become more than friends, which I believe you are aware of."

"Why do you say that?" I blurted out.

"Well those flowers were on the floor to the door of my bedroom, which indicated to me you had been there for some time and saw us in the shower."

I didn't know how to handle this and remained unresponsive.

Rachel and I have decided to share you, if you'll let us. If not, we will make other arrangements."

Other arrangements? What does that mean?

"When she wakes up, you two can discuss this and get it out of the way so we can have a real homecoming tonight."

I guess most men believe having two women is the ultimate and would have jumped at the chance, but I loved Rachel and realized she couldn't love me if she, indeed, were willing to share me sexually with Myrtle.

"Do you want to talk to her first or take care of this problem I have?"

What did she think I was? Superman" I had just spent myself on Rachel and she was wanting what I was sure would be an Olympian effort from me.

I tried to be diplomatic, "Well, I'm a little tired right now. Why don't we wait and let Rachel decide, OK?"

"OK, but while we wait, why don't you have a drink with me? I've noticed it really gets you in the mood quickly." She went into the kitchen to fix my drink leaving me to ponder my predicament.

As we sat and talked, Myrtle told me how hard getting older had been. She had been used to admiring glances from both men and women and lately had very few. Her workout routine each week would have killed me…two-mile runs on the beach each day, aerobics and a special diet. No wonder she looked so much younger. She softened her voice and said, "Look, I know you love her, she's a beautiful woman, but this doesn't mean she doesn't love you. It's just that she needs more, things that I can share with her that you can't. Besides, I haven't had a man in a long time and I miss it.

Rachel came out of the bedroom sleepy eyed and asking for a drink. Myrtle's lack of clothes didn't seem to bother her a bit as they hugged hello. Myrtle informed Rachel of our talk and waited on her response.

"This isn't something I haven't done before and probably never will again, but with Myrtle, it feels right. I love you, but I love Myrtle too, and sharing you with her makes sense to me so she doesn't have to go out and find a stranger to make love with."

There it was, true, so no matter what I say or do, it's going to be wrong. I got up and fixed myself another strong drink, adding a couple of Jack Daniels shooters and soon was numbed out of my mind.

Suddenly, I was fascinated by the possibility. My male ego, fed by the idea that two women wanted me at the same time. Emotionally, I was hurting. I drank enough to see the bottom of two fifths of Jack Daniels, had more sex than I ever had in my life, and an exhaustion that bordered on the absurd.

Both women helped me shower and shave and dress and Myrtle said, "He's in too bad a shape to take the bus, I'll call a cab for him and he can rest on the way back to his ship."

Upon returning to the ship, I realized how sick I had allowed the situation to become. Ted, a shipmate of mine, also had a wife who was having problems adapting to his being away. This was a common ground that bonded us. I explained my situation and Ted didn't believe it at first, so I asked him to come home and have dinner with me next liberty. He agreed if he could bring his wife.

Two days later, we entertained Ted and his wife at our home. Myrtle did not join us for dinner, but brought over dessert just to see what was happening. Rachel and Maris hit it off right away. (Later I found out she had confided almost all to Maris.)

Before the evening was over, we told our wives that we would be shipping out for an extended time. Both women became upset. Maris said there was an apartment for rent next door to her and she sure wished we would move there before our ship left.

The idea was met by great enthusiasm by me. (I'd get rid of Myrtle and we'd be back together again as a couple.) Ted helped me move and even lent me the balance of the money I needed for a deposit. Within that week, we moved bag and baggage to a one flight up apartment across from Ted and Maris. It was larger and had more windows, but a military couple owned it and everything was painted gray (surplus Navy paint). Rachel didn't appear to be upset at leaving Myrtle and that relationship behind. (Little did I know she wasn't.) Along with her new friend, Maris, she started decorating and fixing things up.

Ted and I were on the same watch so had the same liberty routine. Days flew by and everything seemed to be perfect. Rachel was more attentive, Robbie was a happy baby and our friendship with Ted and Maris became close knit. We rarely went or did anything without them. Rachel and Maris were like sisters, sharing each other's clothes and cosmetics.

I naturally was apprehensive after the Myrtle affair, but found nothing to indicate that type of relationship was forming. Ted and I shipped out for two weeks and when we returned, found our ladies on the dock waving and welcoming us home. Rachel was a different person…loving, caring and very attentive. She was dressing differently as if she had come out of a cocoon and was now a beautiful butterfly who needed to be noticed.

My fist sign of trouble was that Myrtle had been visiting while I was gone. Maris had slipped that in a conversation I overheard. Rachel reacted quickly to quiet her when she realized I was listening.

Rachel had not been much of a drinker, so finding all kinds of liquor stocked under one of our kitchen cabinets surprised me. When I questioned her, she said she and Maris had stocked up so when Ted and I were home we could have what we wanted to drink.

Our next movement was for six weeks at sea, so we kissed our families goodbye and went off to do our duty. Six weeks at sea seemed like six months, as we didn't put into port…no phone, no communication at all. I worried only about Rachel and the baby's welfare and looked forward to the homecoming that always felt good. As we slid into port, all the families and friends were standing there waving, then big hugs and kisses of relief that we were home safe again.

Ted and I had pooled our money and bought a beat up old '53 Ford. It used as much oil as gas, but at least allowed the women transportation. The pea green color was easy to spot as the landlines were thrown out to secure the ship to the dock. I hungrily searched for those angelic faces I loved so much and was disappointed when I couldn't find them.

The car suddenly appeared in the parking lot, gasping and squeaking to a halt. Maris was driving. As she got out, I strained to see inside. It appeared she was alone. The hair on my neck stood up. Where was my family? What was wrong? Was Robbie sick again? Ted and I had first liberty, so after the formal stand to and then release, we ran down the gangway to meet Maris. She looked serious and upset. She gave Ted his hugs and kisses and told me Rachel was fine, but didn't feel like coming out and would see me at home. The ride to the apartment felt strange. She had always met me on the dock before. Even when she didn't have a car, she found a way.

As I climbed the stairs to our door, my apprehension increased. The banister was broken in two places and in need of repair. I slipped in quietly in case Robbie was sleeping and found Rachel in bed. She stirred as I entered the room, looked up and said, "Hi, baby. Sorry, but I didn't feel like coming down." As she hugged and kissed me, the smell of alcohol and cigarettes invaded my nostrils. Rachel rarely had a drink if I wasn't home and she didn't smoke.

I didn't say anything as I put my sea bag away.

"Why don't you fix us something to drink? It might make me feel better, honey."

I suspected she was hung-over. "Where's Robbie? I want to see him."

"Oh, he's over at Myrtle's. I didn't want him to catch whatever I've got and thought you'd enjoy us having the privacy."

"Myrtle? You're back with Myrtle? I thought you told me that was over with," I said with a bad taste in my mouth.

Rachel got up and headed for the kitchen. "Let's not argue about this, you just got home. Let me fix you a drink and we'll talk about it."

I gave in and had a few drinks, enjoying the softness of the moment with her.

"Listen," she said, "Myrtle and I are just friends. She loves Robbie and likes to care for him."

Not wanting to argue, I hugged her and put the subject away. We got lost in each other reaching the point where we lost consciousness of our bodies and fleetingly floated above and then coming back down with our toes tingling and our faces flushed with the glow of satisfaction.

The forty-eight-hour liberty went so fast, when I packed my sea bag I felt it was still warm from the unpacking. I had questioned Rachel about the broken banister and she answered, "Oh, Myrtle brought a rowdy friend over and he fell against it, almost breaking his neck."

Naturally, that went over big. Not only was Myrtle coming over, but was also bringing male friends with her. Rachel and I had an intense discussion concerning this not taking place again and she locked herself in the bathroom as I packed to leave.

Ted and I hadn't seen each other since arriving home. His look as we went down the stairs to the car wasn't one of a happy camper. Maris, with tear-stained face, drove us to the ship and was unusually quiet. Ted also had little to say, so I knew something was up.

Seeing the old jalopy wheeze away, Ted and I walked toward the gangway to board the ship. Ted suddenly said with tears in his eyes, "I can't leave now! Tell them you haven't seen me."

"What's the matter?"

Maris has been with someone else. I can tell because she acts guilty and when I asked her, she broke down crying. I can't leave her now. Not like this."

I was stunned. If Maris had been messing around, so had Rachel. It all started making sense.

"Listen, missing ship's movement will only land you in the brig. Go see the chaplain and explain the situation. Maybe he can get you some time."

Ted finally agreed and went aboard with me. Later he showed me the chit (permission slip) which changed his duty from starboard to port watch, giving him another forty-eight hours to resolve his problem.

"Hey that's great, Ted. I'm sure you and Maris can work things out. Here's some money to take a taxi home and surprise her."

When aboard ship, you get into the rhythm of the routine moving through each day with little mental manipulation…sort of like driving a car and realizing you didn't remember the turns on the way. You had driven that route so many times you did it automatically.

The morning of the second day back aboard, after chow, we stood out on deck for money muster and assignments, which were different from duties at sea. Normally in port, it involved paint up, chip out, basic maintenance. Steel ships rust and this is a never-ending battle. The USS Currituck I served on (seaplane tender) was Admiral Bull Halsey's flagship in World War II and if not given extra maintenance, it showed its age.

Hanging overboard on a Bo' sun chair, I heard the speaker crackle and the starting order. "Now hear this, now hear this, prepare for ship's movement. Report to departure stations immediately!"

Something was up; I had not seen the replenishment crew feeding the belly of the ship with the immense provisions we take on prior to departure.

The pace of activity was incredible. I tried to get to a phone on main deck and was too late. The landline had already been disconnected. I reported to the duty officer on the bridge and took over lee helm, my duty station.

I overheard that a PBY had gone down and was sinking and we were going to assist. One of the two pontoons on the Navy seaplane developed a leak and was about to drag it under. With our large, flat rear deck and cranes, we could lift it from the water and bring it aboard for repair.

How long were we going to be gone? What about Ted? He wasn't given time to get back to the ship. These and other questions were racing through my mind as the Officer of the Deck shouted, "Look sharp sailor! Reverse one third!"

The four weeks away and two additional to be replenished in San Pedro for the trip home were ones of apprehension and doubt about what I would find when I got there. I tried twice in San Pedro to call and let Rachel know when I would be home, but no one answered the phone.

The ship slipped into its berth just as darkness was pushing the sun away. I took the long walk to the bus station. I had saved almost all my pay and decided to take a taxi home. This was not normal, but I felt the need to shorten the trip. For some reason, I paid the taxi off a block away and walked the rest of the way, sea bag on my shoulder and white hat cocked to one side.

As I came into sight of the apartments and my staircase, I saw Myrtle leaving with a sailor, bottle in hand. They were in her car and gone before I reached the bottom of the stairs.

Loud music came from my doorway, which was open, and the sound of male voices punctuated it. I placed my sea bag at the bottom of the stairs, pulled my pants up, straightened my lid and climbed the stairs slowly and methodically, subconsciously knowing what I was going to find and dreading it.

As I entered, my mind froze at the sight of two drunken swabbies in my kitchen and four more in the living room. My presence seemed to make no impression whatsoever as one sailor offered me a beer and another commented, "Boy are you late. Take a number there's four ahead of you."

I felt the blood rushing up my neck like lava erupting from a volcano. The tightness of my muscles suddenly relaxed as I inhaled and let out my breath, trying to control my rage.

The bedroom door was slightly ajar. I barely pushed it when a male voice cried out, "Hey, S.O.B., wait your turn, I'm not finished."

He had just pulled his pants down to take them off when I punched him in the breast bone and took him out with a right cross.

Rachel, glassy-eyed, was sitting up in bed smoking a cigarette. She was nude with perspiration glistening on her shoulders and breasts and her damp hair clinging to her throat. "Well, look who finally decided to come home," she slurred.

Suddenly, I felt the air brush my hair from behind as one of the drunks tried to sucker punch me and missed. The patches on their uniforms showed they were all off the "Connie," the USS Constellation, one of the newest and biggest aircraft carriers in the Navy. Being shipmates, I knew they would stick together, so I pushed past the drunk and picked up the old brass floor lamp in the living room. I swung it around my head like a bat and shouted at the top of my lungs, "This is my house, that's my wife and you get your asses out of here!"

I made contact with two of them as the rest scrambled for the stairs. A comment rang through my ears, "Well, she sure doesn't act like your wife."

The first drunk was just coming out of the bedroom and I caught him flush in the face with the lamp, crushing in the side of his face and spreading blood and teeth on the carpet. Rachel screamed and ran to the bathroom and locked herself in.

I suddenly felt sorry for the sailor I had hit and went to see if I could help him. He threw up his hands as I approached. "Look, I'm sorry, I'll get you some help, hang in there." I took my bloody blouse off and stripped down to my skin, using my T-shirt to compress the side of his face.

Movement on the stairs proved to be the police. I explained what happened. The officers looked at each other and one said, "Look, we have to charge you with assault and battery, especially because that guy is hurt bad. An ambulance is on the way, but because you're Navy, we'll turn you over to the Shore Patrol, you'll be held aboard ship until your court appearance."

Rachel was still locked in the bathroom, and I could hear Robbie crying. With the officer's permission, I looked around and located the baby in his basket in the linen closet. He was wet and the stinging red diaper rash was no doubt hurting him bad. I cleaned him up and applied Vaseline and baby powder and finally, with a warm bottle and some rocking, got him back to sleep.

In the meantime, the officers had convinced Rachel to come out of the bathroom. "Ma'am, do you normally keep your child in the linen closet?"

"Only when I party. He's safe in there and it's quiet and I check on him a lot, too." Rachel's response was still a bit slurred.

"Oh, I can see by the diaper rash how much you check on him," the officer said sarcastically. "Did your husband hit you?"

"Oh, no, but I was afraid he would, so I locked myself in the bathroom."

"Well, lady, listen closely. We patrol these apartments every night and if I ever come here again and find that baby in the closet and in that condition, I'll have him made a ward of the state and put in a foster home. Do you understand me?"

"Yes, sir," Rachel whimpered.

Ted suddenly appeared, ran to me and asked if I was okay.

"Sure," I responded."

"Well we just got home and when I saw the police, I was worried."

The sailor I had hurt was being carried down the stairs as the Shore Patrol arrived. The two officers took them aside and filled them in. They came over and said, "Get your mess together, you're going with us."

I got another T-shirt, found my hat and luckily found my sea bag at the bottom of the stairs. I said nothing to Rachel, just gave her a parting look of hurt.

As we climbed into the jeep, the first-class petty officer said, "We are going to take you to your ship, not the brig, if you promise to stay aboard and appear when this paper tells you to."

I agreed and thanked them. I guess they didn't blame me for being upset. Riding back to the ship gave me a chance to decide what to do. I never doubted the decision and started preparation immediately.

I hit the slush fund in Battery Group "A." They loaned you money at 30% to 40% interest. Not smart, but necessary as the airline ticket I got Ted to buy cost almost $500. My next liberty, I took a chance the Shore Patrol wouldn't bother me and went home. Two days had passed. She hadn't bothered to call or come see me and I hadn't wanted to talk to her on the phone.

Entering the apartment reminded me of that night all over again. Myrtle sat at the kitchen table, drink in hand and smoking a cigarette. "Well, if it isn't He-Man. What did you come home for, to beat someone else up?"

I reached out, took her drink, pulled the cigarette out of her hand, picked her up and took her outside to the stairs. I could see fear in her eyes as I said, "We can do this the easy way or the hard way, your choice."

"Put me down! I'll go, but you had better not lay a hand on Rachel or I'll call the police and they'll lock you up again."

I slammed the door and saw Rachel standing in the kitchen, butcher knife in hand and backing against the wall.

"Rachel, I'm not going to hurt you, so put the knife away. Get your clothes packed, your plane leaves in two hours."

"Plane? What plane?"

"Your plane back to Huntsville where I found you and incidentally, I curse the day I did."

"I'm not going back to Huntsville. I like it here and I'm staying in California."

"No, you're not staying here, you're going back. If you want to live in California, you'll have to find a way out here again."

I found Robbie sleeping, as usual the Paregoric bottle was beside his crib. I packed what I could find of his things, placed him on the bed with a fresh bottle and fixed two more for the trip.

Turning my attention to Rachel who had put the knife down and had a couple more drinks, I packed her stuff in two old suitcases and what I couldn't get in, I left.

I put most of her cosmetics in a canvas bag she could take on board with her along with the baby bag. I placed everything by the front door and turned to look at Rachel. "You and I are through. I'll get a divorce as soon as I can and I'll send the papers to your mother's house. I want you to listen carefully how. If you don't get dressed in the outfit I put out for you, I will take you to the airport physically, in your housedress the way you are and leave you there. Your ticket is one-way and not exchangeable. I'll give you a little money to tide you over if you cooper-ate. If not, I'll take away everything and toss it in the ocean, all your clothes and ID. Then I'll call my buddies, the police officers who think you are a whore and unfit mother. I'll tell them I found the baby in the closet again and you'll lose him. Now, get up and get moving!"

Rachel made an attempt to approach me and I pushed her aside. "It's not my turn yet!" I told her.

She finally gave in, knowing I would do what I said. Putting her and the baby on the plane was heart wrenching. I was torn between the love I still had for her and hurt and rage that rolled like waves over me.

I saw her one more time when I passed her on the street in Huntsville. She yelled, "Aren't you even going to say hello?"

"No!" I said, and kept on walking.

Chapter 8

SA'CHI'KO'

After Rachel left, life aboard ship provided the discipline and foundation I needed to get through my depression. We shipped out to Okinawa and I enjoyed the long trip. Our homeport there was a single pier called White Beach, which was comprised of a small Navy base that serviced only one or two ships at a time. Our ship, the USS Currituck, a seaplane tender, was set up for port and starboard watches, so about every other day the crew had liberty.

I didn't take liberty the first few weeks. That way I was able to earn extra money taking other men's watches. This allowed me to pay back the money I owed the slush fund and put some away.

In the early sixties, this area of Okinawa was barren of industry. The major employment was providing support for our servicemen and military bases. Restaurants and bars lined the center street in every little village between bases. The farther from the base, the cheaper the prices.

On the road from White Beach to Naha Air Force Base, there were several villages nestled into the rolling harsh landscape that appeared to be stacked stone and boulders littered with caves. The vegetation was spotty, showing evidence of the devastation of World War II.

I finally took liberty and shared a "kamikaze taxi" with a couple of shipmates. We called them that because, although the roads were clear, they were narrow and winding. Each driver decided he owned it at the time he was on it. Hence, whoever got is front tires in the intersection first had the right-of-way. I still think to this day that the locals paid them to drive that way, because once you arrived at your destination, you definitely needed a drink.

Having been here before, I had learned the tricks. First we pass Village I and Village II and pull up to the Lucky Strike Bar in Na'Ma'Nuee, Village III. Ask any sailor who had shipped out to the Far East and he'll tell you he's been to a bar called, "Lucky Strike." From Okinawa to Hong Kong, I think every port city had one.

I never really noticed what the men of Okinawa did for a living. Most liberty was at night so the view of the country was limited. The primary occupation of the women, however, was prostitution. No, not hookers, but organized efforts built usually into a bar setting. Most bars look alike…thatched or sheet metal sides and roof, wood floors and a screen door. Some had lights and were well lit, but most were not.

The 'Lucky Strike' was one of the better ones. It had 1950's Formica tables and chairs. The big Wurlitzer jukebox was filled with scratchy 45's like 'Blueberry Hill' and 'Hound Dog' and a lot of slow belly rubbers, my kind of music. The new recruits, just out of boot camp and suffering through their first bout of duty at sea, couldn't wait to pick out a girl and get it over with quick. Those of us who had been there before knew to hang back and enjoy the show.

Most bars were set up the same. As you entered, tables and chairs stretched the length of the room with dance floor space around the jukebox. Then at the rear, a bamboo bar ran from one wall on the left all the way to the wall on the right. Decorations were anything from military helmets to white hats signed by the donors draped on the walls like trophies.

The large woman in a huge muumuu was Mama-san. If you wanted something, it had to meet with Mama-san's approval. If you crossed her palm with the right amount, you even got a smile.

I don't remember any air conditioning, just fans swirling the cigarette smoke around. It gave the room its own movement and mystery. The smell of stale beer and wood hibachis still lingers in my nasal memories. The menu, if one got drunk enough to eat, was fish grilled over a tiny hibachi or octopus, which tasted good but was like eating rubber, you had to chew and chew.

The favorite trick pulled on newcomers was they had to buy the girls beers or drinks before they took them in the back (short time $5 or long time $10). The girls would order tomato juice with each beer. The sailors were unaware that the acidity in the tomato juice killed the effect of the alcohol so most girls, if they matched them drink for drink, could drink them under the table. Get a sailor drunk and he loses control of his purse strings and his penis…a bad combination.

I loved to dance. Oh, I bought a beer or two but not any more than that. The girls knew that I knew and danced with me when they could get away. If I ever gave advice to suitors (which I don't) I would say, "Learn to dance and you'll never leave alone. Period." The contact of a man and woman dancing slowly, if done properly, can be as stimulating as foreplay, which it actually is. I don't mean pawing and petting. I mean dancing, feeling the movement to the music, getting a rush over rhythm running through her as she feels the beat and it turns to heat and she is on fire.

Because I minded my own business, wasn't possessive, and let the girls know I wasn't a threat or contributor to their profession, they treated me as someone to spend time with in-between. No pressure, no names, just fun relaxing, drinking and dancing. Oh sure, they all tried to get me in the back room. Some even questioned my manhood to try to accomplish this but, gratefully, I didn't fall into their traps and was referred to as the virgin, among other things by them.

Then I ran smack into a wall. She was new and Mama-san personally introduced her to me explaining the girl hadn't worked before and would I look out for her until she was comfortable with the surroundings and conditions. Picture the pale white powdered face of the most beautiful oriental doll you've ever seen, shiny jet-black hair to her waist and petite figure a ballerina would envy. That was Sa'Chi'Ko'. I was told she was eighteen but suspected sixteen or seventeen. She didn't have the hard worn look of the other girls, veterans of the blanket wars. She spoke very little English but immediately liked my name, and told me so. What a gift! Her gentleness reached out and touched my heart. I asked one of the other girls to translate for me and learned she came from a large family who was very poor…five brothers and two sisters. After much questioning, I learned she had been brought to Mama-san by her father, and a portion of what she earned went to him and the family each month. Mama-san had paired her with an older gentleman of means at much profit. I suspect he gave her the first sexual experience. I learned later it had been painful but he had treated her well.

Mama-san knew what she was doing pairing us up, and allowing me to get to know her meant I wanted to keep her away from anyone else. First, I just bought enough drinks to keep Mama-san from coming over and taking her to another table. Finally, I took her to the back where they had little rooms divided by roll-down bamboo drapes. You could hear everything going on in the next cubicle, but you couldn't see. You'll probably find this hard to believe, but Sa'Chi'Ko' and I saw each other three or four times in the back room before I touched her sexually. At first she didn't understand why I didn't want "washy-washy" where they are required to wash a man's genital area before the act and inspect visually to make sure he's healthy. I finally made her understand that I was incapable of performing under those conditions. Surprise!

Sex, I've always believed, is 75% mental and 25% physical if enjoyed by both parties. With me, it's both or nothing. Her English improved each time I visited and yes, I knew she had been with other men, but the time we spent holding, kissing and cuddling each other brought me back to where I needed to be as a man. I marveled at her gentleness and dress. Most of the girls were in mini skirts and short tops and looked hard wearing the extra makeup. Sa'Chi'Ko' had a natural beauty that defied description and a grace of movement I adored observing.

She surprised me one day and served tea the oriental way. I knew Mama-san was aware of our relationship, as I paid $10 each time so she would allow us more privacy. All good things end. No truer words were spoken; I finally got word the ship's movement was in two weeks. I bought my liberty nightly and burned up the road getting to the bar. Mama-san knew better than I did when my ship was leaving. The night after I found out, I burst into the bar looking for Sa'Chi'Ko' and Mama-san said, "Bo, she's sick and she cannot see you tonight." I questioned what kind of sick and was told she had a chest cold and bad congestion. The next night, with pharmaceuticals in hand, I went back and implored Mama-san to let me see her. The medicine I brought her, Turpenhydrate and Penicillin surprised her, and I could see fear in her eyes at my kindness.

Many a girl has found a mate just to get away from that lifestyle. The government makes it almost impossible, but many military have found a way. Was I so inclined? I believe so, but it didn't happen.

I couldn't wait to see her and even paid the cab driver extra to get me there quicker. I regretted that as he knocked me out of my seat twice.

Arriving, I knew tonight would be special by the smile on Mama-san's face, "Come, come to the back. She much better."

She took me way in the back to a large private room I'd never seen before and left me to lift the reed drape and slip inside. Candles were everywhere and Sa'Chi'Ko' was there in the most beautiful oriental brocade with red trim I had ever seen. She was propped up on a pile of pillows and with a smile that broke my heart, she reached out for me, hugged me hard and cried. I thought she was upset but through the tears, she informed me they were tears of "happy."

Mama-san had told her of the medicine I had brought and of my concern. We held each other and talked about my leaving. She told me she would always love me and hoped I would write her often. She said Mama-san would allow her to spend the night with me if I wanted.

Imagine holding a small beautiful bird in your hands. You're afraid you might hurt it by applying too much pressure. You want to let it know in a way unlike ever before that you think it's beautiful in its delicacy. Sa'Chi'Ko' was like that to me. Ivory white, jet black hair and soft like a newborn baby.

We made love differently than I ever had before. First, just disrobing and laying down facing each other enjoying the electricity of a simple touch, the passion of a gentle kiss and the excitement of the subtle contact. We slowly drew into each other, using our legs as guides and our hands as investigators while our mouths enjoyed that intimate sweetness of new lovers. This was lovemaking that reached inside and touched not just my lust but my appreciation of a woman's gentleness and beauty…it touched me deeply and brought tears to my eyes. Sa'Chi'Ko' questioned me and it was my turn to say they were tears of "happy."

We continued until she stopped and pulled away and let me know she was chapped and needed to get something from Mama-san. Her climaxes had been numerous and quick but, in spite of this, she hung in there with me understanding more than just my physical need. I held her close and we fell asleep.

When I awoke, she was gone. When I asked Mama-san she said this was the best for both of us. I never saw Sa'Chi'Ko' again. Did I have regrets? If someone makes you feel special and adds new meaning and reason for life and suddenly they are not there, yes, I missed her badly, but I knew I was not in the position to do anything about it. Be not so quick to judge, had she been given a different chance to make a living, she would have taken it. I'm the sorriest because she didn't have that choice.

Chapter 9

FEAR

He was always careful getting into his car, checking to see if the hood, doors or trunk had been tampered with. He had been that way since the last case in Costa Rica. That attempt failed only because the seat on the driver's side had an armor-plated bottom, normal for those security conscious and with enough money to buy the extra safety.

He checked the electronic ignition monitor he had installed and turned the key. The 400HP SUV V8 roared to life.

Driving home, he thought about his beautiful wife and the great old house they were in the process of remodeling. Two more months and his early retirement dreams would finally come true. Pulling up to the three-story Tudor, he marveled again at their luck in getting this at the price they paid. Most homes on the street were already on the Historic Homes Registry. With six bedrooms plus the full basement, he and his wife would be able to entertain the way they loved.

The front door resisted opening as all the doors did in this aging structure. He struggled with it and made a mental note to have one of the workers fix it tomorrow.

The house was dark as he entered. His wife was still shopping for the new furnishings soon to fill every room. They had talked over their cell phones earlier and she told him she had a surprise for him.

He looked around room to room but observed only the remodeling clutter and tools. Suddenly, he smiled. She knew his favorite hide-away would be the cellar where eventually a bar, sports room and office would be built. The cellar was unusual in that it had two levels and was as deep as the house was high. A staircase ran straight from the house entrance to the bottom with a landing on the left so you could enter the first level.

The door to the cellar, as usual, was stuck. It swung into the opening so he put his shoulder to it. After the third try, he burst through, observing in the dim light the nails that had been used to nail the door shut. It was in mid-air that he realized the stairwell had been removed...and fell to his death.

The note on the refrigerator said, "Baked custard for you...save me some."

Chapter 10

THE PLAN

After eight years of no raise, double workloads and being passed over for promotion three times, she was ready for this. It was simple. She was second in command to a college preppie who got his position as comptroller through old family ties, not hard word. Although he was smart, his laziness left the platform open for what she wanted to do.

The computer part had been easy; inserting a fictitious service company in and onto the accounts payable software she handles. So little by little insignificant amounts were electronically transferred to the bank account she had set up...leaving little paper trail and hidden among the thousands of service charges the large corporation she worked for paid.

She had been at this for two years and managed to increase the amounts slowly after they were not challenged in the last audit. She now had over $200,000 and was working on a quarter of a million.

Tuesday was payday. She had increased the amounts significantly the last quarter and turned in her notice after building in a delete date, so the fictitious service company would disappear as well as its bank account.

Arriving at the bank where she had set up her account, she asked for the bank manager. She advised him she was moving her business to Atlanta and would like to close the account by taking $100,000 in cash and the balance in an open cashier's check. The manager thanked her for her business and asked if she would consider an affiliate bank in Atlanta to do her banking.

Leaving the bank with that much cash made her uncomfortable, but the cash was important to the plan. She bought the boat tickets with cash, leaving them blank so no one could trace her movements.

She had been to the old Princess Hotel in Freeport in the Bahamas just once, but fell in love with it and the island. She had learned that if one could get a native to partner with you, you could open a business fairly reasonably and enjoy the island life.

Checking into the hotel, she couldn't wait to get downtown to Scorpio's, a local restaurant and her favorite. She had the cashier's check pinned inside her bra and the money in a small briefcase, never out of her sight.

The taxi driver on the way downtown urged her to stop at a new dress shop his cousin had opened. She relented when he promised her a 40% discount and besides, she needed some island clothes anyway. Why not? Entering the shop, she was overwhelmed by the two women who met her at the door and invited her to sit while they brought things to her to inspect. Finally, she broke down and decided to try some things on and brought the briefcase into the changing room with her. Naturally, she stepped out a minute to check in the mirror as to how she looked.

Finally, she had decided on four outfits and a swimsuit, paid for them and left…checking to make sure the envelope holding the check was still pinned to her bra she had to remove to try on the bikini. Dinner at Scorpio's was great. She even met a local with a British accent she might want a fling with later, but not now. She had to get the money settled tomorrow.

Arriving at her room, she threw the briefcase on the bed and undressed. Unpinning the envelope from her bra, she tossed it on the bed and went in to take a shower. Toweling off, she decided to put the check in the briefcase and sleep with them both in bed that night. . She picked up the envelope to put it in the briefcase. Opening the briefcase revealed that the money was gone…but that was impossible! The case had never left her side. The dress shop! How stupid! Well, at least she had the cashier's check. Opening the envelope, she realized she didn't. It too was empty.

She dressed in a hurry and took a cab to the dress shop, closed, dark and deserted by now. She let the taxi go and sneaked around the back where she heard voices and saw lights.

She peeked through the small crack in the shade and saw him counting the money and holding the check up to the two women who had waited on her.

It was her old boss…the comptroller!

Chapter 11

STELLA

When you first see someone who is unaware you're noticing them, they show you a face that's real. Stella was what few women can achieve, the epitome of sultry...waist length jet black hair, cameo smooth skin, a ripe full figure, and two purple shaded eyes that reached out and ate a hole in your heart.

But the first look at her when she was unaware of my effort showed me the future—sadness and depression. Her Cherokee-Choctaw bloodlines gave her a very unemotional look not so much cold, but just disinterested.

The restaurant she worked in was called Lindseys and luckily, it was located right next to Zales Jewelers, 115 Washington Street in Huntsville, Alabama, where I had wound up after I got out of the service. The emotional rage that Rachel had created had somewhat dissipated. Thus, this new, sad, beautiful creature I came in contact with every day at lunch encompassed my every thought and most of my actions.

Waitresses are some of the most abused and underpaid people in the workforce. I've seen them stiffed even after giving great service. Most people don't realize they make less than three dollars an hour unless a decent tip is left.

Being a good waitress—professional, alert, and attentive. If she waited on you once and you ordered coffee, she knew how you took it the next time without asking.

Stella was a whole lot of women. Because of her Indian lineage, she was big boned, but the fullness of that 38-24-36 figure melded the motion and movement of her body into a serenade of sexual fantasy.

When Stella smiled you believed it was for you, not just a public token offered out of necessity. I found out later that she was single, lived with her mother and hadn't been dating of late. I had made several attempts at conversation with her and very courteously had been shut down.

I had just purchased what I considered one of the best looking cars in my peer group at that time. A 1960 Ford Sunliner convertible...white, blue interior, fender skirts and glass packs. I decided to park this new acquisition in front of the restaurant and hoped to get a reaction. This particular evening I had just gotten off work and, with cold drink in hand, approached the car. Under the streetlight with that double wax job and chrome shining, the car sparkled like a diamond. Stella was standing there admiring it and said so as I walked up. "Well that's sure a nice car, does it run as good as it looks?" I started it up and ruffled the glass packs. "Only one way to find out. How about it?" She always reminded me of Elizabeth Taylor, arms under the chest with the right hand straight up by the right cheek.

Coyly she replied, "Well I guess. I get off in a few minutes."

The biggest thing to do in Huntsville at night at that time was drive to a drive-in restaurant and cruise...like the "Oasis" on Governors Drive. It had all the pretty waitresses come out to the car with the tacos on a window tray or a drive-in movie that was only a dollar a car and featured a double. My favorite though was the drive up Monte Santo Mountain. This drive took you way above the city so the night-lights became fireflies and carpeted the valley below.

The drive up the mountain was beautiful. Stella was apprehensive. "Where are we going?" "Wernher Von Braun's home," I said. The German scientist captured from the Peenemünde Complex during World War II had eventually wound up here in Huntsville and worked for NASA at the Marshall Space Flight Center. Most, if not all of them, lived on Monte Santo Mountain in very nice homes. Finding Von Braun's home wasn't hard, as my father had worked with him in research and development. Stella was impressed I knew where his house was and relaxed. Driving down the mountain she told me of her father (Shorty) in Oklahoma who ran five crews of men keeping the oil rigs going. She went on to tell me of her mother, Alice, and what a rough time she had since the divorce. We shared a nice night that allowed us to feel that we knew each other. I kissed her once and found her interested and pleased, but withholding. She was a lady and I felt good about this. Stella invited me over to meet her mother when I had the chance and I agreed. That night proved to be the start of something bigger than both of us.

Stella and I started seeing each other and spending all of our spare time together. We had these friends, Lonnie and Bobbi, who had a gigantic country home over the mountain (Monte Santo) towards Brownsboro. Lonnie worked for the government as a GS-14 but would never tell me exactly at what, but I pretty much figured it was connected to the missile projects, as most work out there was. Lonnie was in his mid thirties, long, lanky, six feet four inches and acted just like a good old country boy in spite of what I suspected was a good Eastern education. Bobbi was a petite woman with energy enough for any three and ready to party. Lonnie asked us to spend the night with them one weekend and to my surprise, Stella agreed.

"Will this room be okay for you both? It's all we've got without relocating the kids," Lonnie said. The room in question was on the bottom floor next to theirs, "Sure, you'll be nice and cozy and if you guys need anything or get lonely, we are just next door," Bobbi gushed. The twin beds weren't my cup of tea, but oh well, any port in a storm.

Stella and I settled apprehensively in for our first night together, talked for a while, then turned off the lights. (The sexual Olympics started next door.) Bedsprings started creaking, headboards hitting the wall, ooohs and aahhhs until finally I said, "Stella are you OK?"

"No I'm not OK. What do you think? Come over here."

Given the resistance to final satisfaction we both had gone through, my trip over to her bed was not one of complete confidence; however I found her wanton, willing and just when I felt her reach what we both had been trying to achieve, she pushed me away and cried out "You've got what you want now leave me alone." Unsatisfied, frustrated I retired to my bed. I questioned her the next morning as we were heading home as to her lack of endurance and her reply was simply, "I don't feel I can really enjoy you until we are married." We got married the following week.

When you marry someone, especially one you've never lived with, you're in for some surprises. Stella and I had found a home with the help of Bobbi and Lonnie, just over the mountain towards Brownsboro. This cinder block, one bedroom, was sparsely furnished and was just the ticket for a young couple like us just getting started. As we unpacked, I noticed a couple of bras laid across the bed with the very tip ends cut out of them.

These holes aligned right where the nipples protrude and I suddenly realized why Stella's breasts always appeared to be bra-less. "Stella why do you cut out the ends of your bras like this," I questioned. "What are you doing going through my underwear," she snapped back. "You can't answer a question with a question and expect to communicate. Now you answer my question and I'll answer yours," I countered. "OK, well if you must know, my nipples are very sensitive and I cut that hole so my nipples don't rub. That bra material makes them sore," she responded. "I just happened to find these laying on our bed, so I wasn't going through your underwear, but based on this I think I will." She grabbed me as I lunged for the underwear drawer and we wound up on the bed. "Make love to me," she whispered in my ear. Every man wants his woman just once to ask this, and I was no different. Ours had, up to this point, been a lovemaking of the moment, stolen places and time. This was to be our first real no rules, no time limit, no worry about being caught or interrupted. I undressed her slowly, noticing that her skin was so sensitive even the slightest binding of the material of her blouse or skirt left a rose-colored blemish which then would fade. Her shoulders were created to be caressed as I drove my head and hair into them and brushed them lightly. She moaned. Her neck had the softness of velvet and a smell that made me hungry for more. As I explored her, she reveled in my attention, breathing hard and caressing the back of my head, stroking my hair. I threw off my clothes and gave her the first daylight look at my manhood. She grabbed for me immediately, but I withdrew, as I knew this moment would be a special one and needed to be grown slowly and carefully. Making love is cultivating your partner's pleasure, and when this is the goal of you both, the returns are enormous. As I traveled down that slim rib cage below those heavy rigid-nippled breasts, I marveled at the pure unblemished whiteness of her skin and the tautness of her stomach. Suddenly her hands grabbed me, pulling me up to her for a kiss. We kissed long and lingering exploring each other as lovers will. "Why did you stop me just to kiss or are you worried about what else I was up to," I asked. "No one has ever been there like that," she whispered. "I want you inside me now." Sometimes the anticipation of something is unbearable, so I yielded and made love to her and we found our rhythms.

Stella and I had gotten married at the same courthouse that Rachel and I had. We both had agreed that a church wedding was not financially feasible, so I went and got the license and we set the day.

Driving down to the courthouse, I stopped at a local florist and bought her a corsage and a bouquet of flowers. "Didn't they have any better than these?" she questioned. "But you've always loved the roses I've gotten you," I responded.

"Yeah, but I wanted red ones not white," she replied and pouted.

"OK, red ones it is." I turned the car around, went back to the florist, and bought some red roses. Handing them to her, I suddenly realized that Stella was used to getting her way and it was a pretty good bet that wasn't going to change.

Arriving at the courthouse, I found that Judge Chardon was going to perform the service, the same judge that had married Rachel and me (what are the odds?). To say I was apprehensive would be an under-statement, but I decided that telling Stella would only exacerbate the sit-uation so I didn't.

Judge Chardon had last seen me four years ago in uniform and weighing forty pounds less, so I figured there was a good chance he wouldn't remember me, although my last name is unusual.

"Well, I see you two youngsters want to get married. Well, I take the act of matrimony very seriously and expect you will too…as I join you as man and wife…wait a minute, don't I know you young man? Haven't you appeared before me?"

"Yes, your honor. You married me four years ago, but I'm divorced and want to marry Stella now," I answered with fear. "Do you mean to tell me you want to have me marry you again so soon? I'll have to see the divorce decree before I do," the judge snapped.

"But sir, I lost my only copy and because it's filed right here on record, I thought you could have a copy brought to you," I nervously responded.

"Sure I can do that, but the only reason I will is so this young lady isn't put out anymore on her wedding day. In fact, you run down to my clerk while I counsel your bride-to-be as to whether or not she's certain about what she's doing," the judge thundered.

Now the judge, I was lax in pointing out, had apparently had a few at lunch and also hadn't taken his eyes off my wife's-to-be breasts. Stella had worn one of those cutout bras of hers and because this apparently was an exciting situation, she was at attention and very much apparent.

You get my drift. The judge took her by her hand and led her into his chambers, closing the door behind, much to my distress.

One and a half hours later found me sitting dejectedly outside the judge's chamber still waiting on my bride-to-be and holding the divorce decree as if I was going to be engulfed in flames any minute.

The judge and Stella finally made an appearance.

"Well, my dear, if you change your mind just call me and I'll take care of it, OK?" The judge lifted her head putting pressure under her chin, "and don't lower your eyes so much as they are so beautiful. You must let the world see more of them," the judge cooed.

The judge walked away not saying a word to me and leaving us both standing in the hall unmarried.

"What's going on Stella?" I queried.

"The judge wants me to think about it some more before I marry you," she responded.

"What…that's preposterous…for how long?" I asked.

"Another hour. He just wants to be sure I'm sure, OK?" Stella replied.

Well for the next hour, we sat in the Rexall Drugstore across the square and had a cherry coke. Finally, an hour later the judge, as agreed, married us and threatened me with legal lightning if harm or distress came to this lovely young lady. He also reminded me that because Stella was only seventeen, he had met her mother when she signed the consent form and would be in contact with her as to whether or not Stella was in fact being treated well. Some days are diamonds and some days are hell.

*   *   *

After going through two more jobs, I realized I needed to learn a trade and took a position as an assistant store manager in a Butler Shoe leased department located in a big discount store named Treasure Island located off Governors Drive in Huntsville. Al Oblshinski was my boss and quickly realized that I was willing to work hard and long hours if he was ready to teach me the business. My goal immediately became the priority in my life. After all, I had to amount to something if Stella and I were ever to have anything. I wanted my own store, not just a leased space inside another discount store, but one of those fancy free-standing ones. Butler's was, at that time, one of the leaders in the shoe business.

Stella didn't like my job. She hated the hours and didn't see why I couldn't find something better. She wasn't going to work and I didn't feel she had to, although I told her many times we would have things much quicker if she did. I had been working for Butler's about six months when my boss took sick for an extended period, which gave me the opportunity to run the store by myself. Not only did I do well, the district supervisor at that time, Ira Kraft, noticed my performance and dropped by the store to congratulate me. I took this opportunity to beseech him to give me my own store. He asked if I was willing to relocate. I said, "Sure." He told me of an opportunity in Chicago. Although not a free-standing store, it was one that did a great amount of business thus giving me a good income. I rushed home to Stella with the great news and was surprised at her attitude.

"Chicago, Chi-ca-go, are you nuts. We don't know anyone in Chicago," Stella shouted.

"But honey, it's a real opportunity. I'll be making good money and think of the wonderful things we can see and do in a city that size," I enthusiastically offered.

"Well it seems you've already made up your mind I guess. Nothing I say will stop you."

"Stella you know I love you and want nothing more than to make you happy. If you won't go I won't, it's that simple."

"Oh, now it's on me. I'm not going to have to hear for years that I stole your chance of success," she shouted. "I have news for you, we're going to have a baby. Are you sure you want to raise it in Chicago?"

"What, I'm going to be a father. That's wonderful! What a minute, you're on the pill. You can't be pregnant."

"Well I am. Bobbi took me to the doctor two days ago and they called and confirmed I am."

"OK, listen. Being new parents is a big responsibility. Let's just put this transfer to Chicago on the back burner and discuss it later."

Stella was adamant about not moving to Chicago. She went out the next day with Bobbi's help and took a job cashiering in a local store. I questioned her as to whether working during her pregnancy was a risky thing. She indicated the doctor had said it would be okay.

The move to Chicago was put on hold. I explained my situation to Mr. Kraft. He informed me I had six months to play with, because that's when the current manager would retire and leave. My thought was there was still hope.

Three months into her pregnancy, Stella miscarried at work. Her depression lasted most of the rest of her life.

Stella and I had many discussions about what if...you know what if so and so had been different. These discussions, sometimes heated naturally, led nowhere. It was time to do something. Stella was sleeping most of the day then running the countryside with Lonnie and Bobbi at night, and I had found out, drinking heavily. I finally told her I was accepting the position in Chicago (Villa Park, Illinois...actually a suburb). Stella said she wasn't going. I told her fine, she could stay and follow me later after I got us a decent place to live.

And that's how we wound up in Chicago (Villa Park).

Chapter 12

STELLA II

Leaving Stella in Huntsville with her mother as I sought our fortune in the Chicago area was difficult, but I considered it necessary if our marriage was going to work.

Flying into O'Hare Airport is a real experience. Luckily, it didn't overpower me but did impress me. In fact, it reminded me of when I viewed the Grand Canyon the first time…they both make you feel small and insignificant in their size.

Finding Villa Park where my new assignment was proved easy. All I had to do was find North Avenue, head north out of Chicago and eventually you'll wind up in most of the major suburbs surrounding Chicago. Villa Park was the home of the re-born non-immigrant Italians who still had ties to the old country and a few other things. Most of the homes in Villa Park, this being the sixties, were priced well above one hundred thousand plus. Most of the working class worked in Chicago and commuted. The rest were retirees.

Resnick's Department Store was unusual in that it was a large discount store competing with the big chain stores, but unusual because it was privately owned by the Resnick family, which by luck, was Jewish. Because my work ethic and moxie were appreciated and recognized by the head of the Resnick family, and although I had been raised a good Catholic boy, I was accepted. Running the 9800 square foot lease department within the Resnick operation, one had to adhere to their ways of doing business and still make sure that you received your fair share of the marketing both in store and outside sources, which was part of our lease arrangement.

My first encounter with Abe Resnick was over just such an incident...apparently the former manager I replaced had been one to lay low and not make waves. The store did well but not because of any direct incentive initiated by him. So, when I took over and started monitoring the actual footage we had been given and the marketing being done, I found some discrepancies. First, our stock room space had been reduced and was causing seasonal style and changeover storage problems...simply put, we had to leave stuff out and discount it instead of simply holding the balance until the next season and get a better price. For instance, bedroom slippers great at Christmas and certain gift-giving times, but not a mass display item year round. Resnick's management had appropriated at least half of the storage room we, according to our lease, were supposed to have. Armed with this and a marketing mistake which had failed to give us the proper size ad space for our department (Resnick had increased the size of their ads by reducing ours) in the last three tabloids I could get my hands on, I asked to meet with Abe Resnick, the head of the store. Initially I was told Abe didn't meet with department heads just our corporate people. I would have to take up my grievance with the store manager who I had already had a run in over the way the floors were maintained. So, I simply informed Mr. Resnick's clerk that I would have one of our chief executives, a Mr. Ira Kraft, call him in reference to the matter. Naturally, I was asked to have lunch with Abe Resnick the next afternoon.

"My boy, my boy, it's so good to finally meet you. I've heard quite a lot of good things. Please sit down and break bread with me." Abe was only five feet seven with graying hair normally unkempt, but neatly dressed and always with a vest set off by a gold watch and chain. He always seemed to be larger than life to me because he never seemed to stop moving. Either his body or his mouth were always active. If you listened you could learn, if you watched you got exhausted.

"What will you have, it's on me. My treat today for taking so long to meet with you," Abe went on. "I'll have whatever you're having Mr. Resnick," I replied diplomatically.

"Bagels, lox and cream cheese with a little crème soda. You think you can handle that, huh?" he chuckled.

"Well to be honest, I've never had bagels or lox, but I love cream cheese and crème soda, so it sounds good to me." I held my ground.

When the fresh slabs of pink salmon, onions, bagels and cream cheese were served from his own deli at the front of the store, I followed Abe's guide and built my bagel with cream cheese and salmon. My first bite was surprising. It was good. I liked it, a fact not lost on Abe. "I buy only the best for my customers, you can tell can't you?" he asked. "The best, of course my opinion is based on limited experience as I indicated, but I knew I could trust your judgment as you want only the best for your customers and lessees," I replied.

"I see right away that you're an observant man, someone who understands that without the customer needs being met and dealt with properly, we need not be in business."

"That's precisely my position regarding our lack of proper placement and size of our ads in the tabloids you distribute and the stock room space you've taken away. It's robbing the customer of the information and seasonal displays that would best serve them," I retorted.

The battle was on with Abe at a loss to explain how our stock room storage space had been abused or how our ads had shrunk…it was news to him and he would see that it didn't occur again. Lunch with Abe became a once a week thing. I grew to learn most of the smart things I know today and later used to be successful in retail business from these lunches. Don't get me wrong. It wasn't always warm and fuzzy. There was the time I rented my own industrial quality floor machine, came in on a Saturday night, let them lock me in and stripped my entire department's floor, then applied two coats of wax. When they opened up Sunday morning late, as usual, the other department heads came over and asked why their floors didn't look like mine. Abe went crazy. He had been maintaining his floors with the cheapest labor, chemical and waxes he could get away with. My one night's work had proved to the other lease departments how it should look. Abe cancelled lunch the next two weeks to punish me, but did hire a new maintenance company to do the floors…which to others were never quite as good as the one I'd done.

My living arrangements at this time were unusual. A lady by the name of Lena Caruso who worked in the ladies fashions department part-time overheard me ask someone if they knew of a room I could rent until I could find an apartment for my wife and I. She indicated she only lived ten minutes from the store and had a room she could rent in her home where she lived with her two sons. Not only was the room great, the food she cooked made me fall in love with real Italian cuisine forever.

By this time two months had bone by and Stella had only written me four times, even though I had written almost daily to describe how difficult it was to find an apartment we could afford in a neighborhood we would be willing to live in. Locals had been helping me, but the apartments we would like were just out of our financial reach. Stella thought I was stalling bringing her out and finally threatened to hop a plane and come out anyway.

A week later, true to her words, I got a call at work. "Well, are you going to make me spend the day at this crazy airport or are you coming to get me." It was Stella and she was pissed.

Getting from Villa Park to O'Hare Airport is a good two-hour effort if you were an emergency vehicle with lights and sirens. Inasmuch as I had to arrange for someone to watch my store…gas up the car and find my way…two and a half hours wasn't bad. She had given me the right terminal but wasn't out there when I arrived. You can't leave your vehicle unattended in those particular lanes so I was in a panic…how was I going to find her and not have my car towed? Suddenly I spotted a sky-cap and motioned him over. After some negotiations and a twenty-dollar bill, the skycap with wallet photo of Stella in hand disappeared inside. The local security made me leave and go around three times before I finally stopped the skycap and Stella (looking mad as a flight of hornets) waiting for me. I jumped out, gave the skycap the other ten I promised, thanked him and loaded Stella's luggage. By this time, Stella had gotten in the car and was sitting stiff and rigid in her seat not uttering a sound. The drive home was about as noisy as a funeral. Finally Stella spoke, "The least you could have done was kiss me hello or don't you need that from me now that you're living with a woman who has her own home."

I was stunned…I had sent Stella a picture of where I was living with Lena with her two sons. Lena was seventy-nine, five feet two inches tall and weighed over two hundred pounds. "Stella, how can you say things like that? You know it's not true. I've written you almost every day and you know how many hours I put in…there is no one else but you and never will be." I pulled over to the side of the expressway and grabbed her. Needless to say, after two months of separation, the fire became a flame and finally a bonfire. We both lost all realization of our surroundings…cars whizzing by, headlights bouncing off the headliner. We were completely lost in each other when a strange blue light finally got my attention. Luckily, I was able to pull up and zip just as the officer stepped next to my fogged up window. Roll down your window sir and let me see your driver's license and registration. Also, do you mind telling me what you're doing on the side of the expressway? I explained to the officer that I hadn't seen my wife in over two months and had just picked her up at the airport…and…that we had stopped to embrace and kiss. "Looks to me like you were a little more involved than that. I thought your car was going to turn over the way it was rocking." His flashlight kept roving over Stella's blouse, which hadn't quite been buttoned up all the way and was displaying to the world and the officer her ample breasts. "Well you're lucky you didn't get hit. Take your romance

home and keep it off my highway," the officer shouted as he walked back
to his cruiser.

After this, Stella was miffed, for when we finally got to the house and
she saw that our small little room was right next door to Lena's room
and we couldn't make noise, she went ballistic. "Of all the stupid things,
how do you expect me to live like this? It's a shoebox. We don't even
have our own bathroom," she ranted. "Let me remind you I told you not
to come here. I didn't have a proper place for us yet, but you insisted
and now you're angry at my lack of preparation." I was upset and close
to losing it. The racket had woken Lena up and she knocked on our
door with the admonishment, "You young people get in bed. Some of
us have to get up early and go to work tomorrow."

Stella and I lived with Lena for three more weeks, then we finally
found an apartment.

During those three weeks, Stella had complained so much about that
two hundred dollar piece of junk I was driving (and to my surprise had
saved every dollar I had sent her), I went out and bought her a 1965 red
Thunderbird convertible (used but only 64,000 miles). It had wire
spoke wheels and a white leather interior. I had told her I had a surprise
for her but not what it was. She was showing her pregnancy quite a bit
by now and looked uncomfortable standing on the porch of the house
as I drove up. But when she found out that big gorgeous convertible was
hers, I think it made her happier than anything I ever did. Chicago is
not convertible country. Good weather comes seldom, and top down
weather is probably on Wednesday once a year. But we didn't care. That
car always made us both feel we were on the way to having what we
wanted out of life.

Chapter 13

STELLA CONTINUED

Having something to provide my new family with some security was my driving motivation. A home, savings account and decent car to drive. Very simple goals that, to my mind, point out a man's success. Oh was I wrong. If all you do in life is drive yourself to gain material things, you're eventually going to be disappointed in life itself. (Be careful what you wish for, you might get it.)

Stella's pregnancy seemed to increase my workaholic madness. When I finally did come home, I was mentally and physically exhausted and totally unable to appreciate what I had, what we had just being together.

Stella's routine didn't vary much. She stayed up late watching TV and slept through to 2:00 or 3:00 p.m. the next day. Washing and house chores were done normally when I was home, so our personal and private times were slim to none. Her pregnancy had made her even more moody and depressed. I suddenly realized one day how miserable and unhappy she had become. No family around her, no friends to share her day with, and the man she decided to spend her life with away more and more each day chasing the almighty buck. I decided to do something about it.

Arriving home as usual late one night, I found her doing the wash. I had brought her flowers and candy as I usually did once a week. My way of reminding her that even though we were apart, I thought of her often. This habit became just that in her mind.

"Hi, sweetheart. Here I brought you your favorite candy and these…"

"Put them on the kitchen sink and I'll get to them later," was her response.

"Let me help you fold those as they come out of the dryer," I offered.

"I haven't fixed you a thing to eat, shall we order Chinese (her favorite thing)?"

"No, if you're not too tired I thought we'd go out and grab something," I cautiously offered.

"Out! Are you crazy? It's going on 9:00 p.m. and you want to take me out to eat? I feel like a bloated cow, haven't had my hair done in weeks, I've run out of makeup and my nails look like hell…and you want to take me out?" Her eyes blazed as she got up in my face. "You're never home, never here and apparently don't need my services in the bedroom either," she went on. "That's why I want us to go out. I want to talk to you about some things I'd like to change and want us to work out," I hurriedly interjected.

"What am I going to wear? Nothing fits, everything I try on makes me look fat," she started to cry.

I took her in my arms and told her that no matter what, I loved her more than anything and wanted her to be happy. If she could find something to slip on, I would take her out and we'd get her some things to wear.

"You mean you're taking me shopping…I'll be ready in thirty minutes." The tears disappeared and that seldom seen smile that I treasured crossed her face.

My campaign to win back my wife's happiness started that night with a four hour shopping spree that left the bank account so decimated that we wound up taking Chinese home.

Hidden love notes on her pillow when I left each morning, calls home during the day (which woke her up most of the time). Once a week I took her out to see a movie or eat. Also, I tried to meet some of our neighbors so we could make some new friends.

By this time, we were living in Melrose Park and I was running nine paint stores (lease departments within Topps Interstate Department Stores). This required me to travel the tri-state area—Indiana, Ohio and Illinois—as they were spread out. My duties as an area supervisor dealt more with keeping managers. As usual in the retail industry, the pay scale was low, the hours long, and the title wore thin very quickly when you had to do a physical inventory each week and keep the open hours covered. If someone didn't show up, you filled in. That meant if one of my managers was out, I was it. I managed not to have to stay away from home overnight, but sometimes driving the expressways at one in the morning the distances I had to travel was stupid. However, my intention was to spend as much time with Stella as possible as the time for the baby approached.

Gary and Pat lived just below us and had become very good friends. Gary worked at Ford Motor Company in the Melrose parts plant and never ceased to be amazed at the hours I put in. They were a young couple five years our junior, but enjoyed playing table games—Monopoly, cards, etc. One night when I came home and found them at my kitchen table, I noticed a very familiar odor as I walked in. Marijuana…they had been smoking. I took Gary outside and asked if my suspicions were true. He confirmed what I already knew and said they wouldn't smoke in their own apartment because of the new baby, so they'd get a sitter and come upstairs to mine. I was furious.

"What about my baby that's on the way. Didn't you ever consider the effect it might have on my wife's condition?" I asked. Gary apologized and said no they hadn't and they would stop immediately. I then questioned him, "Has Stella been smoking pot with you?"

"Only once or twice and we told her it wasn't a good idea. Pat even let her know she quit while she was pregnant and just started back," Gary informed me.

I went ballistic. I asked them to leave at once and never to give my wife dope again. Stella knew the minute I came back with Gary that something was wrong and ran up to throw her arms around my neck to console me. I pushed her away.

"How could you endanger our baby's health by smoking pot? Don't you know how dangerous that is to not only the baby, but you?" I asked.

"I only tried it once or twice and it made me feel good. Don't make such a major case out of it…I won't do it again if you don't want me to," those purple eyes eat into me for forgiveness. I relented and let it go for the moment as our relationship had improved of late. Stella seemed happier, more active and loving. I didn't want things to change. That pot-smoking incident was one that eventually became the tip of the iceberg.

I had changed my schedule as best I could to have some weekdays off to spend some quality time with Stella. She wasn't one to go for long walks, in fact she just plain didn't like the outdoors too much as her skin was so pale and the sun so cruel. So we found that eating out and shopping seemed to make her the happiest. Returning home one Wednesday afternoon she advised me she was overtired and needed a nap. I was going to watch some TV and she asked me to lay down with her. Because of her advanced condition, I knew anything else was out and that she would be asleep very quickly, so I joined her in bed thinking I would sneak out of bed later and see the show I wanted.

"Honey wake up," Stella poked at me.

"What…what's the pro…why is the bed wet? Are you OK?" I sleepily inquired.

Luckily, I had driven the route to the hospital beforehand, so I only made four wrong turns getting us there.

Monique Theresa Banville was seven pounds, four ounces of beautiful baby girl, who had only taken thirty hours to arrive, but was healthy as a horse. Stella was pissed. She had called me so many names in the delivery room the doctor had advised me to leave, so I didn't get to see the actual birth.

"You rotten miserable son-of-a-bitch, how could you do this to me. It hurts so bad…don't you ever think of us having another one," just some of the under-the-pain-of-labor responses.

I was a father and a prouder one never existed. I was scared, apprehensive and bursting at the seams. My beautiful Monique was going to have the best I could give and always know her father loved and adored her. This did not prove to be the case.

A newborn baby changes your entire life. It sure did ours. Stella came home with the baby and appeared to be overjoyed at being a new mother. I assumed that would bring us closer together…never assume.

As usual, I was working morning 'til night leaving in the darkness and arriving home in it. I felt good about making a good living for my family. We were middle income. No matter how we tried however, building a savings account was almost impossible. One step forward and three back. Stella continually pointed this out to me, and I reminded her that all the rest of the couples we knew driving those new cars and going out all the time, were up to their tails in debt that would eventually catch up to them. Stella went into a deeper depression than before. She was asleep when I left in the mornings, apparently got up once to put the baby in the playpen, and then slept in until one or two in the afternoon. I worried about her and Monique constantly. We had heated arguments about the condition of the house (she liked to do her housework at night). I found Monique wet when I came home many times and we had arguments over this often. She indicated she didn't feel well. I took her to the doctor. He said her depression was the biggest problem, although she did have a heart murmur that scared her occasionally.

I had married Stella when she was a curvaceous 120 pounds…she now weighed 143 pounds and as a result was feeling even worse about herself. I remember sitting down to a weekend spaghetti dinner. She had invited the downstairs neighbors over and had the house looking unusually nice. Stella served, and then over her overloaded plate of spaghetti topped with a ton of Parmesan cheese, informed me I had to run down to the store and get some Diet Pepsi. I questioned her as to why she wouldn't drink the regular Pepsi we had plenty of, but she insisted she was on a diet and I would have to go to the store. I reluctantly went, not wanting to have a fight in front of our neighbors. Her diet efforts failed miserably and our ability to communicate became non-existent. I retreated into more of a workaholic than before. The only thing I looked forward to was seeing my super baby Monique. By this time she was walking and talking and a joy to be with. I cherished every moment I was able to spend with her at this age. Her favorite word was "Why?"

I had been fairly successful at the retail business, but I realized that the promotions I had received had simply meant more responsibility, longer hours and days away from my family. I had to do something else. But what? I had, at different times, made in-store announcements for various promotions after which some of my customers would tell me what a wonderful voice I had, that I should pursue a career in broadcasting. I, of course, crossed this off as foolish and went on about my business. However, life takes some funny turns. One night sitting in the living room, I started to turn on the TV and spotted a magazine that Stella had apparently ordered. I picked it up and was about to complain about the money she was spending on her subscriptions to anything, when my eye caught an advertisement for Career Academy of Broadcasting…it shouted at me in large headlines. "Auditions are being held on Wabash Avenue in downtown Chicago for a lucky few to be chosen to attend Career Academy of Broadcasting." If chosen (and if you were a veteran) financing would be provided, plus they would help you find a job in the business. Wow my mind exploded. This was my chance. I ran into the next room and told Stella my plans explaining that broadcasters made good money and that it would be something that few could do this important. Stella's reaction was unexpected. She laughed out loud. I asked her why she found it so funny and she replied, "You have a wife and child to support or have you forgotten that. Besides, you have as much chance at that audition as I have being Miss America."

I think that was when I made up my mind to leave Stella. Instead of at least trying to give my dream a little support, she crushed it, which was not the right way to handle me. She had for years been able to wrap me around her little finger when all was said and done. This time my mind was set. I attended the supposed auditions (just a way to get you to sign up for the course), was accepted and qualified for a V.A. loan that would finance the whole thing. Stella would not go with me to the auditions telling me she didn't feel well. I had left her and her box of chocolates in total bewilderment that I was going through with this.

When I arrived home and told Stella that I had been accepted and would be quitting my job and finding another one so I could attend school in the evenings, she went nuts. Her first reaction was physical. She picked up a lamp and threw it across the room smashing it against the wall.

"You have gone out of your mind. How are we going to live, pay our bills. What am I supposed to do while you're at school? I'm not going to put up with it and I'm not getting a job if that's what this is all about."

I knew I had my work cut out but something inside of me told me I could do this and drove me.

Monique was a blessing. She was the shining light I looked forward to each day. I had found a job at the Ford Motor Company's parts plant in Melrose Park. That allowed me to start work at 7:30 a.m. and leave at 3:00 p.m. This meant I could go home (sometimes finding Stella still in bed and Monique watching TV and playing by herself in the living room). I would take a quick shower, shave and take Monique out to the park where we enjoyed the swings and all the things a father and daughter should. On the walk home a couple of blocks, I always stopped by the ice cream store and got her one. This became such a routine Monique would get herself ready without any prompting. Each day this was our special time and I learned a lot about what went on in my home when I wasn't there. While the cat's away the mice will play.

Children's innocence can sometimes be alarming, especially when you find out that mommy has had men friends over while you've been gone and that she smokes those funny-smelling cigarettes she makes herself.

Stella was a hot-blooded woman when she wanted sex. Nothing was going to deter her. She would find a way. I found this to be a wonderful trait in the early years of our marriage and had some beautiful memories…

*   *   *

Guntersville Dam and Lake is located just over the mountain from Huntsville and in the summer time was the perfect playground for young lovers. Stella and I had impulsively driven there on a sun-filled weekend. I usually didn't have to work. Our funds were low, so we slept in the car and ate on the tailgate. The green lush dense forest surrounding the lake provided enough privacy so that we could take our clothes off and make love under God's canopy with the sun caressing our bodies and a cool breeze providing a temperate balance.

Stella was magnificent to look at…full breasts, small waist, ample hips and that jet-black hair down to her waist. Her skin reflected the sunlight, while unblemished and soft. Her eyes were pools of purple turning slightly gray when she really got upset. Stella loved sex as I did and had the unbelievable ability to have multiple orgasms and continue to try for more. We explored each other over and over trying to find something we'd missed and reveling in the freedom this location gave us. Luckily, we were just getting over an exceptional effort when an older couple happened to pull up (I always suspected their motive was curiosity as I had parked at a location two to three miles off the main road deep in the forest at a small clearing which took some effort to get to). When the car pulled up Stella and I simply got up and slipped on our bathing suits.

"Well," Stella said angrily, "they've just ruined the best weekend we've ever had."

I responded immediately, "Sweetheart don't get upset. I'll see how long they are going to stay." I walked over to the fairly new Ford and found the couple in their sixties staring at us. "Afternoon folks, sorry about the condition you caught us in, but we're newlyweds. That's why we drove in so far off the main road to get a little privacy." I was trying to make a point and be friendly at the same time.

The woman with no makeup and wearing an outfit that looked more likely to be found in church clutched her little purse and stared at me through her spectacles as if I was the creature from the Black Lagoon…nudging her smiling husband to say something.

"Well this is a public preserve and we sure don't appreciate having to put up with this kind of indecent behavior. As soon as we get back we're going to inform the park rangers." To this day, I always felt he said this for his wife, as his eyes never left Stella who was walking back and forth at the car, trying to figure out what was going on.

I didn't miss a beat. "You both should try some sunshine. It would make you feel young again. Nothing like the sun on your skin and the cool breeze molesting your limbs." The Ford fired up and threw debris everywhere as it almost wrapped itself around a tree getting out of there. I guess my choice of words upset them.

As I walked back to Stella she shouted, "What did you say to them?"

"I simply asked them if they'd like to join us," then I ducked.

"Well what are we going to do now, I don't want to go home yet," she cajoled. "I'll figure something out baby. Get your things together right now though. I believe we will have more company soon."

We packed up quickly and skedaddled out of there. Three or four miles down the main road later, we saw the park ranger in an awful

hurry heading back the way we had come…we both laughed hysteri-
cally. "Boy they missed a good show. Your body is so beautiful it glows."
As I said that, Stella grabbed me and almost made me wreck the car.

I suddenly remembered the islands in the middle of the lake were
also densely wooded. The only problem was, they were only accessible
by boat. Luck was shining on me. By following the lake's contour, I
found a boat rental place and Stella was beside herself.

"What are we doing renting a boat and where are we going?" she
snapped.

"Just help me get a few things in the little store there and I promise
you this will be a weekend you won't soon forget," I crowed. We picked
up more picnic supplies, threw our blanket in the boat and we were off.

Guntersville Lake was, and I understand still is, one of the most
beautiful lakes in the U.S.A. It covers miles and miles and is the result
of a large dam built as part of the original TVA project years ago. The
islands scattered here and there I assumed were high points of land not
reached by the dammed water. They too were densely wooded and, as
far as I knew, uninhabited. I had in fact taken the time to ask the man
who rented the boat about this and he had agreed no one lived on those
islands.

The day had turned even more beautiful…the sun playing in and out
of an occasional cloud. It was one of those days you wanted to swallow
and be filled with fresh air and sunshine and with the addition of the
mist of spray created by the boat's movement through the water, life was
good. Stella was in her glory preening as we passed other craft or people on the shoreline. She had propped herself up in the bow with the life
preservers as stuffing and the blankets as cover making the entire front
of the boat look like a divan. She had on a black bikini that showed off
her assets and was posed facing me. As I watched from the rear where I
was attached to the tiller motor control, she started her strip tease. First
letting me just peak at her hidden parts just to get me aroused. Next, she
took off the top covering herself with her arms and then exposing her-

self to the sun intermittently driving me crazy. I was amazed. Except for the bedroom, Stella had always been so modest and ladylike in public (except for the cutout nipples in her bras). She apparently loved the natural setting we were in and felt safe. I knew she was really feeling the wine we had been imbibing when a fast speedboat blew past us with two young couples aboard and she uncrossed her arms and waved causing those large breasts to undulate at if she was dancing. I had spotted two islands and circled both, finding boats pulled up on shore and families having cookouts. Finally, I spotted a small island with a very rough shoreline that was favorable for landing a boat, but appeared to be deserted. I circled it twice and tried to find the most favorable place to pull in. To be honest, if it hadn't been a rental I wouldn't have risked it. As it was, Stella had to get out and help me pull the boat up on the gravel and rock strewn beach. She cut her foot in the process and although small, it bled as if someone had slaughtered a hog. It took awhile and as I never travel without a first aid kit, I was able to stop the bleeding, add a Band-Aid, and after two or three more swigs on the bottle of wine, Stella was back in a loving mood and urging me to grab the life preservers and blankets because she wanted to go for a walk.

Running through the woods loaded down with life preservers and blankets, we both acted like we had been released from jail. There are moments that make memories in life and I knew as we reached a small secluded clearing, this was one of them.

Stella made us a bed and then stripped. Then she did the unpredictable, "If you can catch me you can have me," she offered and giggled.

She had forgotten about her cut foot and dashed like a deer from tree to tree. The sunlight filtering through the overhead canopy provided a marvelous leafy pattern to her nude body. We played like this for a few minutes more until she suddenly became aware of the injured foot again and let me catch her. I picked her up in my arms and carried her back to our makeshift bed, gently laying her down and gazing at her. At that time, I really felt I was the luckiest man in the world. A beautiful woman laid out nude in front of me who loved me and wanted me to make love to her. A day only dreams order—the unreachable natural seclusion of the setting we were in. To this day, I even remember the wonderful and mysterious breeze that rustled the leaves as we exhausted our passions. Of course, the snap of a twig brought both of us out of our surrealistic trance scrambling mentally to try to identify what had made that noise. The fear that we had been observed caused the adrenalin to rush through my veins. My heart pounded from the excitement. We both couldn't identify the cause, but understood without any verbal communication that we both had heard it. We slipped on our swimsuits and raced back to our boat, which luckily was still there, however getting it back into the water was harder. I told Stella to wait and let me get it back in the water. She gratefully did so, observing that it took all my strength to slide the bottom across this gravel and rock beach to achieve success. She crossed and threw our stuff in just as we heard another snap again. The breeze had picked up and apparently was blowing strong enough to cause old tired branches to let go. Hopefully that was so, but we never did know and because of this never repeated the adventure.

*　　　　　　　*　　　　　　　*

When I graduated from the Career Academy of Broadcasting, I had made the most of my time. I realized early on that the school had many limitations that included old equipment, old formats and little on-the-job applicability. Consequently, I cultivated a relationship with Mike Sullivan who was my instructor but also served as News Director at WGRT in Chicago. WGRT was owned by Daddy O'Daily and was an all black station with Mike as the white minority. Because of this, Mike was able to put me out in the field part-time and pay me for any actualities (recorded interviews) that were newsworthy. The Grant Park Riots occurred outside the democratic convention. The Black Panthers were active and the Conspiracy Seven trial was underway. What a great time to be a reporter. I had to make up some press credentials that Mike approved. I received twenty dollars for each sound bite they used. In Abby Hoffman's case it was rough because they had to bleep every other word.

Stella had come somewhat out of her depression and we had improved our relationship. She still complained about my hours but in a different way, and I noticed her care of the baby and the house had improved. I hadn't confronted her about the things I had found out from Monique. I decided to let that dog lie until another day.

Graduation day also meant a job for me. I was one of the few graduates who captured a job right away. I was ecstatic. Stella was livid. The job was midnight to 6:00 a.m. at a country music station in Charleston, South Carolina. It only paid one hundred dollars a week.

"How in the hell are we going to live on one hundred dollars a week supporting two kids," Stella roared.

"Two kids...what do you mean two kids," I said as intense fear gripped my spine.

"I'm pregnant and have been for two months," she informed me. "How in the almighty hell did that happen. You're on the pill." "I quit taking them...I thought you were going to leave me," Stella replied.

"Leave you...when did I ever say I was going to leave you? The thought never crossed my mind. But another baby right now. You're bound and determined I'm not going to get into broadcasting. Well, I've got news. If I have to take three jobs, I'll pay the bills and we will survive."

Stella had purposely gotten pregnant and I hadn't any input on the decision to do so. This probably changed our relationship forever.

     *   ✴   *

Charleston, South Carolina, home of Fort Sumter and claim to the longest retail street in the nation, King Street, was not only a visual delight along the battery, but the epitome of what's left of southern hospitality.

Stella's sister by pure chance lived in Charleston, which helped our situation immensely. Becky took us in and gave us a place to start from, until we could find a place of our own. We found ourselves eventually buying our first home under the 235 Government Program in place at that time. The two-bedroom ranch was located in a subdivision called Roseville in a bedroom community outside Charleston called Summerville.

I went to work at WQSN radio, and soon found I needed more income immediately. Working from midnight until 6:00 a.m. let me sleep from seven until 11:00 p.m. Thus, I could sell radio advertising from the time I got off the air until I went home at 6:00 p.m. Needless to say, it didn't leave much time for anything else. I made more money selling advertising than on-air work and realized right away that the owners in small to medium markets are the only real moneymakers.

Stella and I passed each other daily like two ships sharing the same lock. She made friends, developed social contacts and seemed to be satisfied with life. Our second child was born...Angelique. Where Monique took after her mother, Angelique with her blue eyes and blonde hair, took more after me. I try to remember those times and am frustrated. It was as if all I ever did was work. I can't remember any good quality time with my family. I was so blindsided by my position as a disc jockey and the rapid promotions from small stations to one of the biggest TV and radio stations at the time in Charleston.

WCSC was Charleston's oldest and most prestigious broadcasting facility. They had reached out and hired me away from a station in Summerville. With newspaper ads announcing me as the newest addition, I had worked hard for the recognition. The only problem was I started believing my own press clippings and walked around with an inflated ego twice the size that any man could handle. I was away from home more and more. Stella and I separated for a while. We couldn't communicate anymore…then the worst happened.

Stella and the kids were living in a mobile home by this time, after selling the home, which reduced her monthly expenses. I had agreed to watch the girls while she went to work. She had found a job she loved— tending bar on bingo night at the American Legion. She made good tips, but her addiction to the slot machines (illegal, but put up with by the authorities at that time) left little for her to bring home. Her habit of spending time there, even when she wasn't working, had increased. The outfits she wore to work were a constant nightmare for me. Velvet black hot pants, a deeply cut blouse and boots. Needless to say, she drew so much attention I had to stop going with her, as it just led to trouble.

I had numerous conversations with her about where she parked. She left late at night and although the legion had a big well-lit parking lot, she almost always chose to park next to a fence nearer the building but shadowed in darkness. I counseled her about how vulnerable she would be if someone wanted to rob or rape her. She always rebuffed my remarks, indicating I was paranoid and over reacting. She could take care of herself.

The rain was never ending and had been all day; the sound of it on the mobile home flat roof was hard on the nerves. The wind as usual was up and showing off, blowing debris helter-skelter. The last thing you wanted to do was get in your car and go anywhere. I had fixed supper and cleaned up the kitchen, something I enjoyed when I had the time to do it. The girls were enjoying being with me. We had started a game of Monopoly on the kitchen table…I heard a door slam and immediately got up and went to look out for Stella's car. The parking space was empty and nothing else appeared to be moving but the trees fighting limb to limb to remain erect in the wind. I had just resumed my seat and was determining where I was I the game when I heard what appeared to be a soft tapping at the back bedroom door. We didn't use this door at all so I put my finger over my lips, indicating to the girls to stay quiet. I crept down the long hallway to the back bedroom and heard the soft knocking again. This door wasn't used as the back of the mobile home butted up against a fence, so the front doors had the only stairs. It didn't make sense who would be trying to get in, for that matter who would be out on a night like this unless they had to. Suddenly I heard her voice pleading…"Let me in Bo, it's me, Stella." Stella at the back door…something was wrong! I grabbed the door handle and tried to open the door, forgetting the little slide button on the side. Finally I was able to open the door just enough to see out. It was Stella in a strange yellow rain poncho, the kind you see law officers wear. Rain cascaded over her face as she burbled her request, "Close the hall door, I don't want the girls to see me like this." I closed the hall door yelling at the girls to get a treat and stay in the kitchen; I'd be out in a moment. I applied all of my body weight to the door to push the chain link fence back enough to allow Stella to enter the doorway. Reaching down and pulling her up, I realized she was crying, sobbing uncontrollably. This was a first. Through all our trials and tribulations, I think I had only seen her cry two other times, both during our daughters' births. Stella's Choctaw-Cherokee heritage gave her that control which now had disappeared…my heart stopped. I held her close and knew something really bad had occurred. "Where's your car…what's wrong…what's happened?" The sobbing intensified as I literally dragged her over to the bed and removed the rain gear and wet things she had on. One of her boots was missing which I found quite strange, and then I saw the marks on her face. Some animal had beaten and raped my wife.

When someone is raped, the whole family has been…its effects are long term and, in some cases, permanently damaging to any and all relationships. What most people don't know is how they will react to rape when it occurs to someone in their own family, especially a man's wife. Ask me how I would've reacted before the fact and I'm sure I would have said understanding, concerned, supportive. Instead, after the fear and listening to the details which I forced her to discuss (not something I'm proud of), I got mad…really mad. Mad that it happened…mad that I hadn't been there…mad that she had put herself in harms way…and mad that the police hadn't called me even though she had asked them not to. Mad they had allowed her to come around the back of the home unescorted in the rain…I don't think I've ever been that mad and hopefully never will again.

Stella had told me she was coming out of work with two other people she usually walked out with. Their car was right outside the door. They asked if she'd be okay, said goodnight and drove away. Stella had, in spite of my warnings, parked close to but in the darkness right up against the fence. She walked over to the car not observing anything that would alarm her to what was about to occur. As she opened the driver side door, she felt him behind her…big, black and reeking of alcohol. He pushed her face down on the front seat. She clawed her way across to the passenger's side door and suddenly realized it was blocked by the fence. The attacker, well over six feet and two hundred pounds, hit her until she quit resisting and then raped her. She was found later by people leaving the Legion. They hadn't heard or seen anything but they saw her boot lying outside her car and then heard the deep agonizing sobs of someone crying…then the police…the hospital…and finally coming home to a husband who seemed more concerned about revenge than her agony. Years later I taught over 150 women a rap self-defense course developed out of Boston. It's called W.A.R. (Women Against Rape) and I recommend it highly.

With Stella now a basket case, I decided to pull some personal maintenance. I realized I still loved her and no matter what other differences we might have, right now we needed to be a family.

I knew unless we moved away, Stella would not be able to cope as just the geography reminded her each day of the incident. I called my mother in Oregon and advised her we were going to relocate. She suggested my checking some of the local stations in and around Eugene. I found the idea of moving to the west coast exciting, as there are some great broadcast facilities there. Before anyone knew what was really happening, I landed a job at KWIK radio in Corvallis, Oregon, just twelve miles down the road from my mother. We packed up, rented a U-Haul and off we went, the girls, a black cat named Gypsy, and Stella, only a shadow of the proud woman I had married.

The trip across country took us days and we had numerous adventures—some good, some bad (speeding ticket). But all in all, it gave all of us a chance to re-establish our family; and in spite of the lack of privacy, Stella and I managed to settle the question of intimacy and whether we were still compatible. Let me just say when she decided that's what she wanted to do, I think we set an endurance record.

It rained for sixty-eight straight days…we had been inn Oregon for a year…Stella and I had been taking martial arts training (Okinawan style Chito-Ryu). A sergeant from the local police force had tried to recruit Stella to join when he observed her in a public demonstration we did. She asked me about it. I told her if that's what she wanted to do, I would support it but didn't like it. She had an affair with my martial arts instructor; I found out about it and confronted her. "I understand you and Kerry have been seeing each other while I'm at work."

She looked surprised. "I was going to tell you. It was going to be a surprise. He's been teaching me some new forms and is going to let me do a solo demo at the tournament next month."

"How does he manage to do those forms in that little place he lives in?" I asked sarcastically.

"We go outside on the lawn," she quickly replied.

"Funny, when you go over there no one seems to see you come out except to leave…between the rain and this, it's my turn to be depressed."

I packed up Stella and the girls and sent them back to Stella's mother who had by now moved to Charleston also. I had to work out my notice at the radio station.

After a month, I moved back to Charleston, finally becoming manager of a radio station in Moncks Corner, South Carolina (about twenty miles north of Charleston). The 3,000-watt FM radio station was brand new and its call letters were WTWF (we called it the waterfront). Invitations to its first day on the air were sent out in the form of passports. A big banquet was held at which we kicked off the programming, and because we had invited every significant businessman in the surrounding three counties, I sold over $37,000 worth of on-air advertising, with another $20,000 promised. Betty Roper and Karl Roach were the owners (from Sumter, South Carolina).

Stella, by this time, had become a police officer. After her academy training, she was put directly into undercover work and was instrumental in putting the chief of police of Charleston, at that time, in jail. Needless to say, we saw little of each other, but did manage to build a beautiful three-bedroom brick home in a subdivision called St. James Estates just out of Charleston.

The banquet was an evening affair and I had invited Stella to accompany me, indicating however she would have to drive herself as I would be literally living at the station night and day, getting the new equipment up and running, testing the automated format, and producing all of the public service and advertising we needed to air. I apologized about this situation and Stella said simply, "If you can't take me, then I won't go."

"No, I want you to be there…tell you what, I'll send a limo for you. How's that?"

"Nope, if you can't take me, I'm not going."

We argued right down to the last minute about this with no better results. As I left to go to the station for the live-in marathon, I decided to do as I always did, try one more thing. I ordered a big bunch of her favorite roses and wrote her a love letter reiterating my feelings and reminding her that my next stop would be station ownership and to hang in there and it all would pay off.

The two-day live-in at the station was the nightmare I had expected and more. Murphy's Law (whatever can go wrong, will go wrong) was rampant—electronic gremlins attacked our audio, transmitter problems beyond our young engineer's capacities, software problems with the mainframe computer that had to run the whole thing, faulty wiring in the old frame house we had fixed up to use as a studio. Plus, my production needs had to be done renting a studio from another competing station whose manager, luckily enough, I had worked with during our formative broadcast years and he gave me a break. To say I was stressed not only would be an understatement but absurd. Luckily, Betty and Karl, the owners, were handling all the banquet arrangements. Otherwise, I would have really gone crazy. Finally, the frenetic evening arrived.

The owners had, through their contacts politically, managed to utilize the state's major utility company's country club-like facilities on a beautiful lake. This 20,000-foot plus building was surrounded by lush, dense woods adjacent to an immense lake. Our arriving guests that evening were impressed. If you want to make money, you have to look and act successful. The banquet hall had been turned into a majestic offering. Instead of white table clothed banquet buffet tables, I had suggested they buy some royal blue velvet bolts and use that instead. With the real silver services and candelabras the effect was most pleasing, as the food has been catered by one of Charleston's finest restaurants, "The Chapel," (five star downtown by the marketplace) epicurean elegance and champagne. A heady evening for everyone. Then Stella arrived unannounced!

I had just worked the room for the fourth time shaking hands, stroking vanities, building new relations and selling, selling, selling, all the while running to the phone every so often to check in with my staff to see if they had double checked everything. God forbid we hit the broadcast switch and nothing happened. We had coverage from radio and TV stations and newspapers throughout the state, not because of our size but our novel marketing and format. The old frame house on the highway leading into Moncks Corner had been turned into what appeared to be a bait shop or quaint fisherman's camp with a land-locked pier built as a porch all around it, complete with tie up stations and rope. "The Waterfront," as it was called, also had a new untried format. All music played twenty-four hours a day had to deal with love lost, love found or love renewed. It didn't matter how big a hit it was. If it didn't deal with one or all of those, it didn't get played. Also, anytime you didn't hear music, you were listening to the sound of the ocean and sea gulls.

Cocktails and champagne flowed, food was consumed and I stepped up to the microphone for the moment..."Ladies and gentlemen my name is Bo Wyley, manager of WTWF the Waterfront (applause), the dream of my owners Betty Roper and Karl Roach of Sumter, South Carolina (applause). It is with great excitement and pleasure I give you your new radio station's first sounds. This is the Waterfront." (Loud voice behind me) "Well aren't you going to introduce me?" It was Stella in all her radiant glory. Jet-black hair piled up and off her neck. Heavy black eyeliner and lashed, a form-fitting black silk gown with exposed cleavage almost to her belly button. The black spike heels were set off with rhinestone diamond want-to-bees. Her lips appeared to be purple, which brought out here eyes even more. "Well, yes...dear ladies and gentlemen, may I present the woman who has done without me and many things so tonight would be a success...my wife Stella." (applause) "Now without further adieu, here's the Waterfront." (Ocean sounds followed by music)

I had made sure that because the sound systems in buildings are not designed for quality stereo sound, that stereo receivers set only to our frequency with the largest speakers I could find were in every room our guests would have access to, even the bathrooms.

I turned immediately to thank Stella for changing her mind and coming and she was off to the bar for a drink. I started across the room to make contact with her and naturally was grabbed by numerous guests and our owners congratulating me on the way things had come off and the sound of the station. Consequently, I didn't have a chance to make contact with Stella for at least another forty-five minutes...she was hot. "Well, I see you can talk to everyone else but me. Why did you invite me if you're going to ignore me?" I was just going to respond when one of the largest multiple location car dealers in the state walked up and grabbed my arm. "Son, I can see I should've hired you to promote for me. So this is the little woman you've been hiding...woof...if she was mine I'd never let her out of my sight." (This helped immensely.) "Mr. Richards, let me introduce my wife Stella, who I'm sure appreciated your sentiments." Richards put his arm around her waist and walked away with her in deep conversation. I didn't see Stella again for an hour. "Hey, I've been looking all over for you. Where did you get off to?" I asked.

"Dicky took me for a ride in his new car and showed me all the new gadgets it comes with," she slurred.

"I'll just bet he did," I leaned down and whispered in her ear. "You've had too much to drink. Let me get someone to drive you home."

"Why don't you drive me home," she slurred again.

"I have to stay here, I'm working. It's my job to sell these people some advertising so we can pay our bills."

"Well, if you can't take me home, I'll get Dicky to," she pranced off before I could say anything else. Naturally, that's when Karl (one of the owners) grabbed me and introduced me to a lady who owned a chain of wig shops (wig imports) who was interested in signing a long-term commitment with the station if I would help with her overall advertising and promotion program. It took over two hours at the end of which I had a $10,000 contract in hand and a promise of an additional personal income as consultant to the tune of $1,000 every three months. You must realize the mixed emotions I was experiencing...exhaustion, pride, excitement and disgust at my wife's conduct. I searched high and low for Stella or "Dicky" (Mr. Richards) with no success. It was 1:00 a.m. and I had to go on the air with my first show at 6:00 a.m., so I made my excuses, tried to call home (no answer), climbed back in my car and drove to the station to let the staff go home.

The fiasco at the dinner party became a sore on our relationship. She never accounted for her time that night and I quit trying to get her to talk about it. An uneasy truce is descriptive of the following months.

Through all of this, the girls were my delight. When Stella wasn't there, normally I was. We had hired a terrific mature lady named Suzie to be our housekeeper. She was great with the kids and able to stay over most of the time we couldn't be there.

This particular day I had left early to do my show and dragged in after a day of sales and personnel problems around 8:00 p.m. Stella wasn't home yet. The kids were still up so I decided we'd have a marshmallow roast around the fireplace, something we hadn't done before but one of those things I wanted to do. Monique was seven and Angelique two years plus. Suzie got everything ready while I showered and got comfortable. I cautioned the girls how dangerous this was and not to try it or they could burn themselves or the house down. Sometimes you have to give kids information even if you think they might be too young to comprehend. Ninety percent of the time they will surprise you. The evening was cozy; the girls fell asleep asking for one more toasted marshmallow. Suzie helped me get them to bed. I had just poured a shot of Jack Daniels and was putting the lights out when Stella's car pulled up. She was right in the middle of her late shift. What was she doing home? When she came in, she was surprised I was still up and said "Hi" as she passed me and headed for the bedroom. I finished my drink and followed suit. When I entered the bedroom she was sitting on the bed still dressed and crying. Something was really wrong. "Stella what's wrong…talk to me."

"Well you're going to find out anyway. I'm going to get fire," she sobbed.

"Fired, what for? They can't just fire you for no reason. There's a review process and everything. Tell me what happened."

"The chief had me in his office since six this evening about an investigation of my partner, Vince Sutton, and I." She went on, "They found out that we spent time in a motel when we were supposed to be on stakeout watching this suspect, but we knew exactly where the suspect was and if he went elsewhere our snitch would have called us. I don't know why they are making such a big deal out of it."

My mind was racing...let me get this straight. She was in a motel room with her partner when she was supposed to be working...she doesn't think it's a big deal and apparently was more concerned about losing her job than me being upset over her behavior. I was surprised I wasn't angry...just hurt that we had come to this.

"Let me see if I understand, you and Vince went to a motel apparently more than once when you were supposed to be working...and you don't think it's a big deal...you're a law enforcement officer...you were on duty...of course it's a big deal." I took a deep breath. "What did the chief say he was going to do specifically?"

"He told me there would be a review, but that my job with law enforcement was over," she was still crying.

"What were you doing with Vince in those motel rooms?" (I couldn't believe I was asking the obvious.)

"We were both tired and worn out from the case we're working on and decided to get some sleep."

"Is that what you told the chief?" I sat down next to her.

"Yeah, although I don't think he bought it." (And she thinks I will...amazing.)

Stella was not living in the real world anymore and I knew if she lost her job as a police officer, she would be a basket case for the rest of her life. I did something that was probably one of the hardest things I've ever done in my life. I set up an appointment to see the chief who I had come in contact with in my broadcasting endeavors.

"Chief, thank you for seeing me right away. As you probably have figured out already, it's about my wife and the situation you found her in."

"Well, Bo, I appreciate your coming in but I can't discuss that issue as it's an ongoing investigation and then will be reviewed." The chief's response had a warm tone.

"I understand you can't discuss this, I only ask you to listen and consider the circumstances and stress Stella's been under. I haven't been a husband or man to her for a long time…Vince Sutton has been helping me try to solve that problem."

"Vince Sutton is helping you with your marital problems. That's why he went to a motel with your wife?" the incredulous tone indicated his disbelief. "Well, Bo, if you love her that much to come in here and tell me a cock and bull story like that, I guess I'll take a harder look at keeping her and letting her spend a couple of years on patrol. What do you think about that?"

"I'm not adverse to her being a police officer. Since the rape incident, it has seemed to give her strength and self-worth. I just have to figure out a way to fix our marriage, if that's possible."

"Well thanks for the input, Bo…but I still don't think for a minute that Vince Sutton is the answer."

"Thanks, chief. Can I tell her she still has a job?"

"Yes, tell her to report to my office tomorrow around 10:00 a.m. and we will make it official."

When I went home and told Stella, she went off like a rocket. "What in the hell is wrong with them? I put the former police chief in jail. I'm one of the best undercover detectives they've got…patrol…patrol…I won't do it. I'd rather die."

She didn't thank me for going to the chief. I realized I still loved her however…and didn't know why, I just knew it hurt and hurt bad.

A couple of months went by. Stella and I drifted farther and farther apart. We went through the motions for the kids when we were home, but that was it. Stella became more and more silent and depressed, even Monique and Suzie asked me what was wrong with her. I did make an effort for her to see a doctor. She just looked at me and said, "I'm fine.

You're just trying to find a reason to put me away." I called her sister, Becky, and explained the situation and asked if she and her mother could help. They tried with no luck. Then the situation turned really bad.

By now, I had most Saturday mornings off and enjoyed being home with the kids, sleeping in, and having a normal breakfast. I had drunk a little bit too much the night before and was really foggy this particular morning.

I felt it before I realized what it was…cold, metallic and shiny as the morning sun forced its way through the blinds and into our bedroom…reflecting off the silver sides of the .38 caliber silver plated police special pressed against my temple. At first, I naturally assumed I was dreaming, but as I closed my eyes again, I could still feel the pressure against my temple. That cold chill of terror that tightens up your buttocks, travels as an electric current up your spine and explodes in your brain happened…and I was wide awake…reality can do that, especially when it comes wrapped in a Colt Cobra .38. I tried to move my head off the pillow to see who was holding the gun. The pressure increased and then I heard the sobs. "I know what you're up to. You're going to have me put away, declare me insane and take my kids away…well (sob) I'm not going to let you. I know you're going to get me for going to bed with Vince…that's why you didn't get mad and yell at me…(sob, sob)," Stella took a deep breath. As she had been talking, I had snuck my hand up close to the right side of my face. I was lying on my left side. She had the gun pointed aligned with my right temple just behind the ear. "Stella listen to me…I loved you enough to go to the chief and save your job for you…I want you in my life not out of it, and as for the kids, they need you now more than ever. We've both made mistakes…I want to work things out, not put you away." This was a selling job I couldn't lose.

"Don't give me that bullshit. I know you've just been waiting for a chance to get me." I suddenly locked my hand around the gun putting my thumb between the hammer and the chamber. She wasn't able to squeeze the trigger, but tried as we rolled off the bed onto the floor in the struggle. Finally, I was able to gain control of the gun. I picked her up off the floor and threw her back on the bed.

"Listen to me very carefully. Don't move from that bed an inch...I'm not calling the cops...I don't want my daughters to know their mommy tried to kill me. Stay right there and don't move and both of us might get out of this without someone getting hurt." The fear in her eyes was evident as she pulled the blankets up over her.

The rest of that morning was like a dream sequence. I packed what I could carry in two suitcases, mostly clothes, and threw them in my old beat up 1961 Chevy Impala (I called it my fishing car, although I seldom went fishing.). There was plenty of money in the joint account that Stella and I shared, so I left her my checkbook, kissed my babies good-bye, and drove to the radio station. I called the owners beforehand, informed them I had an emergency, and asked them to meet me there. Betty and Karl had been good to me; I didn't want to leave them holding the bag. They met me at the station. I explained I had a family crisis without going into specifics and had to leave town. They thanked me for my effort on their behalf and tried to talk me out of leaving. I left Moncks Corner and drove for an hour before I finally broke down and pulled over. The woman I loved wanted me dead. Nothing else seemed to matter. I thought of my girls, started to turn back and rationalized they were better off with Stella in a home they were used to instead of dragging them into what I wound up doing. I continued to drive north not knowing where I was going and not caring. My insides were hurting so bad, pain of any kind was a relief. I didn't set eyes on Stella again for a long time...but that's another story.

Chapter 14

ANITA

Working six 'til midnight at a station in Fayetteville, North Carolina, gave me time to try and get my feet back under me. I missed my girls desperately but not their mother. I hadn't heard from Stella, although I had sent the girls letters. When you work late hours when most normal people are going home to their families, you come in contact with some very lonely people who listen to the radio just to hear a friendly voice. If you realize this, you're able to relate to them and all hard-working late shift workers too. I took request calls and started recognizing that most of the same people called me each evening. Those were the days when radio was live and you could make non-liner note comments and take requests. Thus, become a human being, a real person to your listeners. I guess my sorrow and loneliness came across, although I tried to keep it professional. In those days, all disc jockeys had radio groupies who called just to see if they could score. If you were smart you didn't alienate these, just teased them enough to keep them listening. You didn't want them for enemies because there had been numerous incidents of vindictive callers who felt they had not been treated well, stalking and even doing damage to personal property of the air personalities they were upset with. In my current frame of mind, I wasn't ready to date and was very careful about taking any relationship past a telephone one. Then there was Anita…

"Bo, these flowers arrived for you. I told them you didn't come in until six tonight, but they left them anyway." Smokey, the DJ I relieved each night handed them to me.

"That's OK Smokey, probably one of those groupies trying to request something they're not going to get," I replied.

"Be careful, last time a woman sent me flowers she had told all her friends we were engaged including her parents. Her father came down to the station with fire in his eyes and informed me that messing with a fourteen year old was a criminal offense. It took me some talking to convince him and his family I had never laid eyes on that person and that I was happily married with three kids."

"I'll be extra careful, thanks for the heads up, Smoke."

The card with the flowers said simply, "Don't beat yourself up. There are ten people waiting in line to do it for you. You're a sweet caring man who is great company to me every evening. Thank you for that," signed a listener.

The fact the card was unsigned and with no phone number gave it credibility with me, so on the air that night I thanked my unknown listener and asked them to call in so I could thank them personally. That was the first time I talked to Anita.

"WFAI radio, this is Bo, how can I help you?"

"Bo, my name is Anita. I'm the one who sent the flowers."

"Well, I'm so glad you called so I could thank you one on one. They are beautiful and most appreciated. I must ask you what you meant by the message however."

Anita paused…"The poetry you write and read every night is poignant and sensitive and when I listen to it, I realized that you're deeply upset over something that's happened to you and beating yourself up mentally over it. Of course I could be wrong."

"Well I don't discuss my personal life with my listeners normally, but I will tell you I'm in the process of a divorce and miss my two daughters, which is probably what you sensed."

"That's a coincidence. I'm also just divorced with two kids. I guess we both share some of the same feelings." Anita had a break in her voice as she said this.

"Listen, Anita, thanks again for the flowers and concern. I have to go but I'll play you something special."

"Remember as I do, there are people who care about you and if you need to talk, just ask flower lady to call you over the air and I'll call." She hung up and I sat there for a moment thinking what a sincere and caring person she seemed to be. She hadn't left a phone number or hit me up for a date. She had just been nice to me. That was unusual. Not that others hadn't treated me well, but with this one phone call Anita had touched something…maybe both of us being in the same hole of loneliness and divorce depression. The show went well that evening, plenty of listener participation, which made the time go by quicker. Before I knew it, midnight took over and my relief was opening the studio door. I gathered up my stuff and was headed out the door when the other jock informed me I had a phone call. I told him to tell them I was gone, when he informed me it was the flower lady.

I went into the studio next door and picked up the phone.

"This is Bo."

"This is Anita. What are you going to do now?" (Oh, oh! She is going to turn out like all the others.)

"Why what did you have in mind?" I asked sarcastically.

"Well I don't want you to take this wrong, but I'd like to have a cup of coffee with you and talk a little."

"It' a little late isn't it? Besides there aren't very many places opened right now where you'd really want to go to."

"No, I was thinking you might come over to my house. The kids are in bed and I'm wide awake and can't sleep…but just to talk…nothing more." (Well, she is for real.)

"Are you sure it won't put you out?"

"It's fine. I'll give you directions. I live only five or ten minutes from the station."

"If you include an egg sandwich in that offer or some cookies, I'm on the way."

She gave me directions and I made record time getting there. It was a small two-bedroom asphalt-sided two-story that looked tired, surrounded by a chain link fence that had seen its better days too. I knocked softly only once and a very petite black-haired Spanish woman answered, "Bo?"

"Yes, you must be Anita." I noticed how clean the place was as I followed her into the kitchen. Anita turned suddenly and said, "You don't look a thing like you sound."

"I've heard that before and never know what to say. I'm sorry I'll try harder next time or whatever."

"No, no. Don't get me wrong. I'm pleasantly surprised. I pictured you as heavier and dark complexioned."

"Well, I'm Scotch, Irish and French. People have told me with reddish-blonde hair, blue eyes and build that I take after my Irish heritage in looks, French inclinations in relationships and the Scotch shows up in my temper."

In the light of the kitchen, I finally got a good look at Anita. She appeared to be in her thirties, five feet one or two, very trim small figure (couldn't tell too much more as she had on an oversize sweat shirt and jeans.) Her hair was dark brunette. When the light caught it just right, it had dark red highlights. Her eyes were large and dark black liquid pools. Ones easy to look into and get lost. She apparently had some Indian in her (later I found I was right…Apache), but her Spanish ancestry was the predominant.

Anita bustled around the kitchen as I said, "Don't go to any trouble. I was just kidding. A cup of coffee will be fine."

"What are you usually doing this time of night?" she asked.

"Well that depends. If I want a drink to help me sleep, I drive over to the Double S Bar and catch one or two scotches. If I don't want a drink, it's straight home, a shower and maybe a video. Not exactly the exciting life most people think I lead."

"I don't know. I got the impression you weren't a party person. Do you take cream in your coffee?"

Anita and I sat and talked ourselves into morning. She suddenly jumped up and said, "Oh my, look at the time. I've got to get the kids off to school and get ready to go to work myself."

"I'm sorry, I didn't think about you going to work. I'll get out of here. Don't want to give the kids the wrong impression."

"My kids know I don't sleep around, so don't worry about that."

"That's not what I meant. Thanks for the conversation and company. I enjoyed myself."

Anita turned and gave me a deep look, then kissed me with a passion I was surprised at.

"You're a sweet man, Bo. Thanks for letting me get to know you." I left feeling pretty sure I would be seeing her again and liking the idea.

I had done a stupid thing. I left without getting a telephone number. Luckily, I remembered the law firm she worked at as a legal secretary. I called and left a message asking her to call me. Two days later she did.

"Bo, sorry it took me so long to get back to you, but I had a family emergency and had to go out of town. My sister was in an accident."

"Is she going to be alright?" I asked apprehensively.

"Yeah, she's just shaken up because the guy that hit her died and she knew him. What's up?"

"I thought I'd take you out this Saturday if you could go."

"Oh, I would love to, but can't. My son has a peewee soccer game and I don't miss those."

"I'd be glad to come along if I was invited."

"You would...well, ok, meet me at the house at nine and I'll fix breakfast before we have to go."

"I'm looking forward to it, thanks!"

That Saturday was fun. More than I had in months. Being around family again made me feel like part of one. Billy, Anita's son, was seven and smart as a whip. We hit it off right away and between his input and Sarah's, Anita's girl, I found that they hadn't met many of Anita's men friends. I felt special and told Anita how much I appreciated the trust.

"I'm very particular who I allow around my kids. You're very good with them, but be careful. They give their hearts willingly like their mother and can be hurt easily," Anita imparted.

I suddenly realized looking into those intense dark eyes that Anita was falling in love with me…was I falling in love with her or her family. I was mixed up and avoided calling her for a few days. I had the number this time and called late one evening when I felt the kids would be in bed.

"Hi, I didn't want you to think I forgot you. I just had to work some things out in my head."

"That's alright, I understand. I do want you to know you've been the topic of conversation with my kids. They think you're cool…would you like to come over for a drink or coffee after work tonight, or do you have other plans?"

"No, tonight would be fine. I'm looking forward to seeing you."

That evening, Anita and I made love for the first time. We had a few drinks and talked…suddenly she kissed me with that upsetting passion I had experienced before. I looked into her eyes and said, "If you're going to kiss me like that, we need to be somewhere private." She grabbed my hand and took me to her bedroom at the rear of the house. The kid's rooms were at the other end, so we couldn't be heard. The black and brown comforter and pillows to match were unusual, and I liked the rest of the room too. Anita lit some candles, took off her clothes and slipped under the covers. She was so quick I still was getting my shirt off. She watched my every move, not taking here eyes off me. I had kept myself in pretty good shape of late. Losing a little weight at six foot and one hundred-eighty pounds with a flat stomach, I felt good about myself and enjoyed her gaze.

"You have a nice body, Bo."

"So do you, what I got to see of it," I teased.

"It's been a long time since I was with a man, you'll have to go slow."

"That's my favorite thing to do, go slow." I pulled the covers away from her feet and started kissing her toes and massaging the undersides, then I worked up the legs kissing and caressing until she threw the covers away and grabbed my hands, guiding them to where she wanted them to be. The first time a couple makes love it can never be re-created. It's a permanent memory that should be special. If it's rushed, panicked and too physical, it's lust, not love. I am lucky because I was taught to make love and enjoy it.

Our lovemaking became periods of passion and exhaustion as we enjoyed the magic…that special electricity that passes between two people in love. The afterglow never left us as we showered together in the morning and I snuck out the back before the kids got up. I called her after I got home and thanked her for making me feel special.

"Bo, as I told you, it had been a long time for me. I was amazed at how gentle you could be and how strong you are. Very few men have been able to keep up with my energy," was Anita's response.

I don't know quite what it is, but when I feel myself getting emotionally involved, instead of baking up and taking a second look, I tend to jump off the cliff with both feet and no parachute.

Sarah, who was fourteen. and Billy became my life. I took them to the movies, shopping at the mall and even amusement parks. (I say even because I hate those rides, but I went.) My life started revolving around Anita and her family. My job became secondary. I knew something was going to have to change, but also resolved not to even think about marriage. I was on the air one evening when Anita called and said she wanted to come over to the studio to see and talk to me. This was highly unusual, so I knew something serious had happened.

Anita showed up about fifteen minutes before I was due to get off. The minute I laid eyes on her, I knew she was upset and had been crying. I hugged her and told her nothing she would tell me was going to make me walk away, that I loved her and would support her in any way I could. She relaxed and asked if we could go for a drink. Then she'd tell me what this was all about.

The Double S Bar was owned by a couple, Larry and Sally, who thought that anyone in radio put his or her pants on differently. From day one they had treated me special and made sure that if I wanted privacy I got it. Anita and I had been dancing there a couple of times and Larry had made a concerted effort to keep groupies away and let me enjoy the evening. That evening Sally gave me a big hello and I let her know right away that I needed some space. We retired to a table way in the back and ordered our first round. Anita had been tense and I could see by her body language she really didn't want to tell me what she was about to…

"Bo…I'm in big trouble…big enough to send me to jail. My sister is going to take the kids, but…but they'll need more. You've been so good with them and they listen and respect you. I need you to help me explain to them what's happened and that I will still be their mother and we will be a family again…but I'll be going away for awhile." She broke down and started to sob so hard she couldn't get her breath. Sally ran back to see if she could help. I nodded no and she went away.

"Anita, take a deep breath and start at the beginning. Why do you think you're going to jail…what did you do?"

"I helped one of the lawyers at the firm divert funds for his own use…and once I did, he blackmailed me to continue and gave me some of the money."

"Who's idea was it originally?"

"He came to me a year ago and asked if I could help him out. He said it would just be a two-week loan he'd replace and no one would know.

I knew he'd been having money problems and being married with two kids, was up to his ears on his mortgage and bills."

"Were you having an affair with him?"

She looked up at me, surprised at my question and replied, "Yes."

"Are you still having an affair with him?" Anita reached out and grabbed my hand. "No...no...no...ever since we...I told him I wouldn't see him that way anymore and I wouldn't help him get any more money."

"So you're afraid he's going to involve you if he gets caught?"

"He's already got caught...the investigators from the district attorney's office were in our office today with a Warrant of Search and Seizure for all our records."

"Do they know you were involved?"

"I write the checks and get the accounts. Of course they know."

"But they haven't arrested you yet."

"No."

"Good, how much money are we talking about?"

"Two hundred and forty thousand dollars," Anita said the amount as if she was spitting it out.

"Whew almost a quarter of a million, how in the world did you think he was going to be able to pay that back?"

"He did the first time, but it was only twenty thousand, and because he paid it right back I trusted him when he needed more."

"Have you discussed this with the other partners in the firm?"

"They won't talk to me about it...I've tried."

"How much money did you actually receive?"

"Well I added it up the other night and it's almost ten thousand," she became hysterical again. I put my arm around her and forced her to take a sip of Jack Daniels straight.

"Calm down, Anita. Do you trust me?"

"Yes," she responded.

"OK, here's the plan. You go to work tomorrow morning and I'm going with you. It's time someone played hardball on your side of the bat."

"Oh no, they will think you're involved. You'll be bringing suspicion on yourself."

"Don't worry about it. I've been in tighter situations than this. Let them take their best shot."

It was settled. I met Anita at her office and asked to see the senior partner (informing his secretary that I had information I would share with the news media that would put his firm in a bad light, but I wanted to discuss it first with him). I knew which buttons to push. All of a sudden, his schedule permitted him to se me. I was ushered into a conference room. At the table were three not just one of the firm's partners.

"Gentlemen, I am going to skip the introductions and niceties and cut straight to the chase. First I'm not a lawyer, I'm a radio personality who happens to be a new friend of one of your female employees. A hard working single mother who lost her husband and was left with two kids, an old house and a mortgage. She's worked for this firm for over five years and only received one raise. No, this isn't about a raise…put your hand down sir until I finish…it's about sexual harassment by one of your partners. It's about intimidation, coercion and manipulation. It's about this firm's reputation. You've thrown her to the wolves from what I understand. She's asked for your help. She received less than $10,000 of the almost quarter of a million stolen from that trust. She only took that under duress of blackmail threats. This situation needs to be rectified. I make no threats, just promises. My appearance here today should prove I have no fear of accusations of personal involvement. I will do whatever is necessary and use whatever is necessary to get some justice for this lady. Yes, she did help steal money, but why, what were the circumstances. Listen to her gentlemen and ask yourselves if you really want the public to hear her story!"

I gave them no chance to respond or interfere with my indignation. I stormed out of the office, not even stopping to say goodbye to Anita. I had given it my best shot. I knew I hadn't scared them that much, but my intention was to make them investigate further and then make a decision based on what was best for the firm…which after all was an investment (they will always protect the investment first).

Doing my show that evening was difficult. I was mentally pre-occupied, which you can't be and do the correct thing. After starting my third record at the wrong speed, my program director even called me and asked if I was okay. I told him I wasn't feeling good, but would be able to finish the shift, which he heard with relief because he would have had to come in to relieve me. I hadn't heard from Anita and was worried I had done the wrong thing. Just as I was leaving the station, she called.

"Bo, I need to see you right away…come over to the house, but please park a block away and walk in…no one is to see you come in so use the back way, OK?"

I agreed, realizing by the strength of her voice that something had changed. I parked one street away and went to the back door knocking softly. She opened right away. The place was pitch black. "Turn a light on or I'll break my neck," I complained. "No…no lights," she insisted, guiding me to her rear bedroom by feel. Anita sat me on the bed then lit a cigarette and started pacing back and forth in front of me. All I could really see was the orange glow of the cigarette, as it appeared to have a life of its own floating in the air.

"Bo, listen carefully, I don't know what you did today but it turned that whole office upside down. I've never seen people scrambling and moving so fast. The senior partner called me into his private office one hour after you left and told me I didn't have to worry about being arrested anymore, that the matter had been taken care of. He thanked me for my hard work and apologized for not listening to me earlier. He said I would be getting a raise until my promotion. Can you believe that I'm going to be promoted to an executive assistant to one of California's biggest attorneys? They're moving us to San Francisco, all expenses paid. They are even transporting my car. It's incredible, but I had to sign a disclosure that gave a description of the theft and the fact that I would be willing to testify in court against the partner involved. They did tell me it was for leverage and were pretty sure it would never go that far…however, I am not to tell anyone about this agreement or details of my promotion, especially you. I could lose everything if they knew I told you. I asked them why and they said it would appear that they had bought me off and that you might get upset over it. They told me to tell you I was moving to San Francisco and didn't want to see you any-more…but I can't. You can get a job in radio in San Francisco and move there. Then we can be together again and start a great life."

Anita's dissertation blew me away. I had hoped to be successful enough to keep her out of jail, but this…this was absolutely overkill. I could only surmise by their actions that the firm realized how liable they were and that this was a way of getting off cheap. I also gathered that the attorney that Anita was going to work for probably had some investment in the firm she was leaving, thus they could still keep tabs on her.

"Anita, first let me say I'm very happy for you. I think this will be a great move for you and give you and the kids a clean start, but I can't move to San Francisco. I've got some baggage that prevents me from ever relocating to the west coast again…no, no, don't interrupt me let me finish. Yes I love you, but I don't think I'll be able to get married again and that's what you deserve…someone who hasn't the baggage I do…someone that will give you a stable and secure future. That doesn't describe me. Please don't ask me to go as all I'll say is no and you'll cry."

"Bo, after what you did today for me and my kids I'll do whatever you want."

"Anita, you deserve another chance at happiness…I won't tell anyone about this." (It's years later so I felt it was long enough not to hurt).

Anita and I saw each other under the cover of darkness a couple of times more. Telling her kids goodbye tore me up more than telling her. I lost track of her and the kids. I hope they finally found the stability and happiness they deserve.

Chapter 15

BETTY

She'd had a tough hard life. Born to a sharecropper's family, she lived most of her formative years in poverty. In rural North Carolina in those days however, they didn't know they were poor. Oh, she knew most of the kids she went to school with had more, but there was always food on the table and a roof over their head so life was what it was. She was turned out to the tobacco fields at an early age and, under the blistering Carolina sun, her age accelerated as the heat baked and baked. Her father only knew farming in those days and because he worked so hard and got so little, drank too much and played cards when he could. He was mean when drunk, yet had a heart of gold when sober. She married young just to get out of the fields and away from the farm. The man she married was cruel, uncaring and abusive, eventually beating her once a week just for the hell of it and not permitting her to go anywhere without him. He gave her little or no money for groceries and didn't allow her to work. When she became pregnant and gave birth to their first son, that abuse caused him to be born brain damaged and he had to be institutionalized. She became pregnant again and gave birth to Tim. She finally stood up to her husband one day, running away with her new son to her father's where she knew she'd be safe. Her father and mother had split years ago, her mother running off with another man leaving her babies with a husband incapable of understanding all their needs. She worked in the fields again bringing in the tobacco and earning pennies for her backbreaking efforts. Finally, she got a job in a factory. She moved into her own mobile home and, for the first time in her life, had somewhere near a normal life. She had come through all of this still country-girl fresh, not needing a lot of makeup and hairdos. Her 39-22-36 figure covered by her ever-present tight jeans and western blouse were crowned by big brown eyes and a smile that would melt your heart. Her shoulder length hair was a combination of reds, golds and browns from her years in the sun. She could dance the legs off a table and loved it more than any other woman I knew. Her southern slow North Carolina dialect reached out and wrapped itself around you, never harsh to the ears. This is when I found her...

I had taken a job at WFMC radio in Goldsboro, North Carolina, as the morning air personality. The station was modern country and owned by the Bosley Broadcasting System, the same company that owned the last station I had come from in Fayetteville. As usual I was on air and then selling the rest of the day just to make a decent living. I wanted to buy a new car, so for additional income I had taken a job on the door at a local watering hole called the Wagon Wheel. The club, one of the most popular at that time in Goldsboro, home of Seymour Johnson Air Force Base, was owned and operated by Big Bill, a retired steel worker who through my radio show I had met and we had become fast friends. I had spotted Betty a number of times and because I was working or on a date (a man cannot work and not play), didn't ever really get the chance to talk to her. The Wagon Wheel was about 10,000 square feet of club, almost half of that wooden dance floor. The two bars were busy from the time we opened until we closed at 1:00 a.m. serving up ice-cold red-eyes as fast s they could pour them (draft beer and tomato juice in frosted mugs.)

I watched Betty dance many times before I asked her for one. She turned me down. That shook me up. I didn't get turned down. (She told me later she did this on purpose, even though she really wanted to dance with me.) I couldn't get her out of my mind and asked her to have breakfast with me after we closed. I got shot down again. Betty came with a group of girls and left with them. Sometimes not with all of them, but usually with at least with one. I never saw her come in with a man or leave with one. I became fascinated with not only how pretty she was, but why she wouldn't have anything to do with me.

It was a Friday night and the crowd was bigger than normal. The usual redneck locals, Air Force servicemen dressed in their 'I'm a cowboy look,' and the hard working factory workers just off shift and giving their weekend a jumpstart. Betty and her girlfriends had come in early so they could get their favorite table close to the dance floor. Bill had taken me aside and asked if I would help Ralph as a bouncer tonight. I asked him why he thought Ralph couldn't handle it and he let me in on the fact that a couple of locals he had banned from the club because of trouble were sending some troublemakers in tonight and he wanted to be ready. I agreed and grabbed the lead-bottomed half pool cue hanging by a rawhide thong on a hook on the wall. I slipped it under my jacket in my pants in the back. Bill carried a gun but wouldn't let anyone else. This equalizer however had, in the past, been just that and Bill's place had a reputation for no trouble. If some started, we could handle it.

I worked the door until the regular got there and started drifting among the tables checking in with some I knew, patting the back of some I didn't...a good bouncer can spot trouble brewing and nip it in the bud before it becomes out of hand. Two guys arm wrestling on a table for beers was just that kind of signal. One guy had already been beat twice and his friends were giving him a hard time for being beat by what they described as an Air Force punk. I could see Larry's temper was ready to explode and I had seen that happen before. It had taken three of us to get him to the floor and four to get him out the door. I gently eased myself over. "Now you guys know Bill doesn't allow this. If he catches you, he'll bar you for a year and you boys don't want that. Tell you what, I'll buy the next round so you boys can cool off and if you can't, I'll take the loser for free drinks for the rest of the night."

"You mean you'll take the winner right, Bo?" one of the guys said.

"Nope the loser. I figure if he's lost, he'll be too tired and I might have a chance of beating him. My momma didn't raise no fools…" and I laughed. They all knew me and knew I hadn't ever started anything, but had finished a few. That had surprised them and they seldom after that ever messed with me. My joke had relaxed the situation. One of the contestants finally said, "Looks like we'll have to put this on hold. Besides, I'd rather drink right now than fight anyway."

I motioned one of the servers to set them all up with a red-eye and caught Big Bill's eye. He sauntered over for a how do and took me aside. I explained the situation and he told me I did good, but we better keep our eye on them. I told him I would.

Later on, the same table was getting really rowdy. They had all gotten real drunk, and it was time for them to leave before chairs and tables started flying. I gave the high sign to Ralph. He grabbed a couple of the larger male servers and we surrounded the two tables. "Gentlemen, it's time to call it a night. Why don't you guys take this up the road with a couple of six packs. This place just isn't big enough…you guys need more room to party…" The group looked around and realized we were serious and helped each other out the front door with some preening and prancing and a few remarks. It had happened so quickly and quietly that, unless you were seated right next to them, most of the club never knew what happened. The most dangerous time is after something like this incident, because drunks get vindictive and come back for more. Big Bill (they called him that because it was a fact he stood six feet four and weighed well over three hundred pounds, and even though in his fifties, he was still a handful) relieved the doorman in case some of the troublemakers tried to get in again. I kept an eye on him. About thirty minutes later, I noticed him walking one of the ones we threw out before towards the door. He had him in a bouncer's thumb lock with his arm bent up his back. I was half way across the club and I had a funny feeling Bill might run into trouble in the parking lot. I was too late. The guy Bill had, twisted out of his grasp outside. Someone hit Bill up side of the head with a beer bottle and then the one who tried to get in, smashed Bill in the face. Bill wore glasses and the glass from the lens cut his eye badly. When I got there, I saw two guys running away and Bill on the ground bleeding badly. I stuck my head in the door of the club and, in spite of the noise, let everyone know Bill was hurt and needed help and so did I. Bill was well liked so the club emptied out in no time. All I remember after that was chasing the two to a Wendy's up the street, losing my pool cue club in the process while I was running.

One chose to hide inside while the other went into a karate stance and invited me to take him on. I had studied martial arts for years and knew that I was out of breath and out of shape and that I probably would get one shot, so I better make it good. I pulled the most unexpected trick in that situation, feigning a kick to my face and then allowing myself to fall down while continuing the kick now in an arc to hook him in the Achilles tendon at the rear of his ankle on the foot supporting most of his weight. This was effective because his feet went out from under him causing him to land on his head on the concrete, taking all the fight out of him. The other one came out to help his buddy and made a mistake in walking right up and over me as I was trying to get up off the ground. He walked up to my face with his legs straddling mine. The rest wasn't pretty. Suffice it to say he wasn't much use to his girlfriend for a long while.

I hadn't realized that Betty had been with the crowd from the club that had run down to help. In fact, I later found she was dead behind me when I took on the first guy. I was just pulling myself up after pushing the guy laying on me now in a fetal position with his face looking like someone was using a vacuum from the inside on it.

"Are you alright, Bo?" Betty asked, helping me to my feet.

"Other than realizing I need to lose a few pounds and work out more, I'm fine. How's Bill?"

"I don't know. I got here when you did. Let's go back and see how he's doing." Betty grabbed my arm and we walked back to the club together. While walking, I asked her, "I've tried to get to know you a couple of times. Why the cold shoulder and why wouldn't you at least dance with me?"

"Because I thought you only cared about yourself and were way out of my league. I'm just a little country gal trying to make it. Besides, I have a son and most men don't want to have anything to do with a single mom, except of course to use as a one-night stand. Well, I'm not that type. The man that has me has to work for it and truly care about me."

"Whew! You tell it just like it is don't you."

Betty stopped walking and looked up at me. "I'll always do you that way if you do the same." She put out her hand.

"It's a deal," I said and shook. (First time I ever shook hands with a woman on a deal.)

We went to breakfast that morning and I learned about her life. I asked if maybe she could go fishing with me at Surf City this upcoming weekend. She said no…that her weekends were for her son and father who she spent time with on Sundays. I suddenly said, "Why don't you bring Tim. He probably would love to fish and I'd love to get to know him."

Betty gave me a head cocked-to-the-side funny look and responded, "You mean you want Tim along? This isn't just your way of getting in my pants?"

"You know I still can't get used to dealing with a woman who says exactly what's on her mind. I think you've summed up the situation precisely." Betty turned and started to walk away then stopped, turned and said, "I made a deal with you. I'll speak my mind if you will. I'll let you know if we're going. I have to ask Tim."

Betty never called me so I took off for Surf City alone. The Surf City pier (destroyed recently by a hurricane) was an old one reaching almost half a mile out into the ocean. If you paid twenty-five dollars a year for a King Mackerel permit, you could fish from the end reserved for King Mackerel fishermen. The regular bottom rig fishermen used the sides of the pier. It got pretty interesting when we got a big fish on and had to play it back along the sides to get it in close enough to rope gaff it in. Most of the time I went up Friday nights and caught big blues for bait, then went to sleep on the end of the pier so I could catch the sunrise, which is best when fishing for big kings. Thus when Betty did show up Saturday morning, I didn't have a place for them to stay and had to rent one. The Medlin family had owned the pier for years. I had Charlie on live on my radio show in the mornings, so getting a room was no problem. They had a bait and tackle shop connected to a restaurant at the landside part of the pier. One of the best meals I ever had was there. A fresh, just out of the ocean minutes ago mess of spots fried crisp with ice-cold cole slaw, hush puppies and ice tea.

Tim was what I expected. Six years old and inquisitive as hell. Every sentence seemed to begin with why or what. With his blonde hair and personality, people immediately assumed he was my son and made a big deal out of him. Betty looked great. Although her legs were thin, they were muscled and toned and with those white short shorts and blouse tied across her flat stomach, she made a picture with her hair reflecting the golden rays of the sun as it blew in the breeze. I spotted them just as I got my first hit, so I was busy for thirty minutes before I landed my first big king (twenty-seven pounds) and threw him up on the board to steak him out.

"You didn't call me so I didn't think you were coming."

"Tim talked me into it. He just wouldn't leave it alone and wore me out." Tim looked up at me and said, "What's cha going to do with the fish now, Bo?"

"Well, Tim, I'm going to chop off his head and cut him up into steaks so we can eat him."

Tim jumped up and down and shouted, "Can I help do it…can I…can I please?"

I looked at Betty. She nodded approval and Tim and I steaked out the king and placed the steaks in plastic sandwich bags, then placed them over ice.

That weekend was wonderful. I bought Tim his own rod, reel and tackle box with some bottom rigs, and showed him how to fish telling him that if he became good, I'd get him a King Mackerel rig like mine and he could fish with me. Betty and I enjoyed each other's relaxed company.

"Bo, you're not what I expected you to be at all."

"What did you expect…like everyone else a swinging party-going playboy?"

"That pretty much sums it up," Betty replied. "But I still don't understand how you walked away from those babies of yours. Don't you miss them?"

"Of course I do, but the situation with their mother hasn't changed. In fact, just before I left Fayetteville, she and her new husband paid me a visit one night and threatened to take me to court and take away my visitation rights unless I didn't increase the amount of child support I was paying. I told them if they didn't have those big boat payments to make with the child support money I was sending every month, maybe the girls would have something."

"You need to go to court and get them," Betty said adamantly.

"I already looked into it. My attorney told me I didn't have a chance in hell of going into a Charleston, South Carolina court and relieving a mother, much less a law enforcement officer, of her kids."

That evening was interesting. I had gotten all of us one room with twin beds. I let Tim and Betty get in bed, and in the darkness undressed and got into mine. About thirty minutes later, I felt a hand brush my face. It was Tim. He whispered, "Thanks Mr. Bo for everything. I had a really good time." He then disappeared back to his own bed. I always wondered if she put him up to that…either way, it made me feel good. Sunday morning she and Tim had to take off and go to Mount Olive where her father lived, as the whole family (as most do in the Carolinas) got together for potluck, normally outside, on Sundays.

"Listen," Betty said, "if you get done early, come on over to Emmett's. There's always food left over and I think you'd like to meet him…especially after sending him all this fresh fish. He'll go crazy…it's his favorite."

As they got into the car to get on the road, Tim came and gave me a big hug with no prompting from his mother and then waved all the way down the road. I think I fell in love with Tim before I did Betty.

*   *   *

Mount Olive, North Carolina, doesn't even have its own zip. It is so small. But its claim to fame is the Mount Olive Pickle Factory, which has produced some of the tastiest pickles in the world. (You don't want to see how they're made, believe me.) Betty's brother, who eventually became the chief of police, was a high school football star whose nickname was Scooter. Consequently, when I packed up early and arrived in Mount Olive, Betty's father, Emmett, was easy to find.

Emmett had remarried and had some more kids—two boys and a girl. By this time, both he and his wife had health problems and were unable to work, so the kids either got married or were living at home and bringing in a little more income. The house was a rental—southern style with a porched front, gable roof and some gingerbread. It, however, was built in the thirties and the wiring was, to say the least, suspect as well as the plumbing. I had stopped by my house in Goldsboro and cleaned up. I love white so I had slipped on my white leisure suit (popular at that time) set off with white loafers. To say I got some hard looks when I got out of my car in front of Betty's father's house was an understatement…next door neighbors went inside and brought the old folks out just to see who was visiting. (Later Emmett would remind them I was on the radio.)

It was fairly hot this particular summer's day, so the fans were set up everywhere (no air conditioning). I walked towards the backyard where I heard all the commotion, through the front door which was open, and passing through it from the living room to the kitchen ran smack dab into Emmett with a bottle of bottled and bonded corn liquor (not the homemade they make). He whispered, "You must be Bo. Betty's been telling us about you. Thanks for the fish. Listen, you want a little taste? I try to keep it hid from the kids, but if you're so inclined, have some."

Emmett at this time was in his sixties, bald headed, five feet four and wore glasses. His hands were large and calloused from all the years of abuse.

Emmett picked up a jelly glass off the kitchen table that had resided along side what appeared to be a gallon jug of ice tea, blew it out and proceeded to fill it up with the corn liquor. He then handed it to me and picked his glass up with what appeared to contain the same as mine. "It's good having Sunday company." He tossed down the glassful like he was drinking tea. Well I wasn't going to insult him and make him drink alone. Down the hatch went mine, although I do remember not being able to swallow for a few minutes afterward. Emmett asked me to sit and talk with him before we joined the others. I agreed and that's how I wound up on my back, passed out colder than mackerel. My brand new white suit (which was stained from something on the floor I couldn't get out and never wore again) looked like it had been used to clean the floor. They tell me I slept peacefully for over two hours. I picked myself up (embarrassed as hell), fell into my car and went home.

Betty called me the next day to see how I was doing and to thank me for the weekend. I apologized for my deportment and she giggled. "You're not the first one Emmett's got plowed and won't be the last."

"You mean he did it purposely?"

"Sure, he takes a nip or two now and then, but yours was the real thing, his wasn't." I could hear the concern in her voice as she went on,

"Some people get mad at him for his practical jokes and won't come back to the house. You're not that kind are you?"

"Nope, you invite me next Sunday. I'll be there." I couldn't believe I agreed to go back.

That week went by and I got absorbed in my work. As usual, I had three remotes (on-site broadcasts) plus an exceptional amount of sales, which then turned into additional commercial production. (I wrote, voiced and produced each of them.) I called Betty twice and she wasn't home, so when Friday slipped up on me, I realized today was the day they promised me they'd have my car ready. I had purchased a used low-mileage 1963 Pontiac Grand Prix. I then took it and had the motor and transmission rebuilt. The engine had half again the horsepower, and the car had a new muffler system that made it sound like what I call Hollywood. While idling, it was a pussycat, but when you put your foot in it, just from the sound you knew it was more than stock under the hood. The mechanical didn't take long…just two months, but the re-do of the interior (white pleated and rolled Naugahyde) plus a gold metal flake (the original color) special paint job, had been in the process for three months. Today I'd finally bring her home and the best thing, it was all paid for to the tune of over $3,000. Some people thought I was crazy putting that much money into a used car. I didn't. It made a hell of a lot more sense than going into debt for a new car (never have liked payments). It was mine and I doubt there was another one like it. I went by Gary's Body Shop and picked her up…of course every man wants to show off his new car, so I drove it to all the local watering holes I frequented. The last one I stopped at called "The Den" was located on the outskirts of Kinston, North Carolina, about eighteen miles from Goldsboro. It was a real dive. I didn't come here often and remembered the last time I had picked up a woman and taken her home, but I couldn't remember her name. As I walked into the darkness from the sunshine, my eyes couldn't adjust quickly enough. As I ordered my beer in the blind, a voice I vaguely recognized attacked my ears. "Well, well, look who finally decided to allow us the pleasure of his company again, Mr. Bo Wyley." My eyes finally gave me enough vision to see her sitting at the bar. She was in her late twenties with pale skin, red hair down to her small waist and two of the largest breasts on that small A-frame I had ever seen. She's the one I had gone home with last time. I had gotten so drunk and she offered to drive me home. Christ, I couldn't remember her name. "You're trying to remember my name aren't you? Well, that would be a trick. I never gave it to you. We were too busy doing other things." (She got up and ran her hand into my open shirt.) "And I definitely remember it was good."

I had a few beers and showed off my car to a couple of people I knew and then took the redhead for a ride. She finally told me her name and that she had tried to call me a couple of times and couldn't get through. I heard myself say before I realized what I was saying, "Well, I'll make it up to you. Why don't we go out tonight? I'll buy you dinner and we'll go some place dancing."

Her name was Virginia and she got so excited, I thought we were going to have sex right there on the spot. I dropped her off at "The Den" and told her I'd pick her up that evening.

Life is good was the thought going through my mind as I drove my restored Pontiac over to pick up Virginia. She met me at the door looking like she just stepped off a magazine cover with a green Greek-drape dress that matched her eyes and made her hair look on fire. I had decided to take her to Goldsboro's favorite barbeque place for dinner. Wilbur's Bar-B-Que is still doing open-pit hardwood fired barbeque and has been since the early forties. Chicken, pork, whatever turns you on; they do it and do it best.

Darkness had just laid its coat over as I headed for Wilbur's. A station wagon blew past me trying to beat the light and lost having to stop too quickly. The three little faces in the rear window were thrown backwards and then returned to their positions to press their sticky hands and little faces right up against the glass, so they could make funny faces at the man and woman facing them in their shiny car. I think I felt the danger before I was actually aware of what was happening. The blinding lights in the rear view mirror...the sudden quick look up at the oncoming car that wasn't slowing down...the inclination to turn the wheel and floor it and the realization that I couldn't...the steel grip on the steering wheel as I stood on the brakes staring at those little faces. It all happened so quickly. I think the driver of the station wagon heard the scream of the tires of the oncoming car and moved through the light just as the old uninsured Ford Galaxy hit me at what they figured was forty miles an hour. The heavy Pontiac took the licking and kept on ticking...still running even after the collision. I reached down and turned off the ignition. Then I remembered Virginia.

The collision had knocked her down and under the dashboard, as neither one of us was wearing seatbelts. Her legs were up around her chest. She was literally stuck in a fetal position. It took the rescue crew a few minutes to help her out. She was bruised but basically unhurt, only scared as hell. I didn't want to get out of the car. I didn't want to see what I already knew...my beautiful car that I'd had one day was trash. The rescue crew helped me out and I saw the young drunk kid who hit me being carried to the ambulance. I turned and took in the devastation. The heavy old Ford had hit my rear end perfectly square, as if it had been aimed. The entire rear end from the bottom of the back window to the taillight had been bent upwards at an almost forty-five degree angle. My car looked like a locust...that was it, a giant locust with its legs hunched up. I was sick to my stomach as the police officers wrote their report and advised me the kid did not have any insurance. It seemed like a couple of hours before they finally told us we could go. We both had refused to go to the hospital. I decided to see if my car would still run and, to my surprise, it turned right over. The lights even worked, although the ones in the back pointed upward a bit and some of the lenses were missing, but they still worked. My license plate was imbedded in what appeared to be a metal sculpture. One of the police officers walked over when he heard the car start up and said, "Wow! Sounds like you have something really special under there. Too bad about the accident, be careful getting home."

Home, the last place I wanted to go was home. The accident had occurred just three miles from the Wagon Wheel.

"Virginia, I'll take you home or we'll stop for a drink. Are you up to it?" I asked.

"I'm going to be a mess in the morning, but sure, I could use a drink," she was fussing trying to get herself presentable. I wasn't thinking at all or I never would have gone to the Wagon Wheel. I had planned to take Virginia out to another club, so what happened didn't. The best laid plans of mice and men ran through my mind because, just as we hit the front door, there sat Betty and she even started to get up and greet me until she realized Virginia was with me. She gave me a hurt look and turned away. Virginia and I went to the bar and had a few drinks when suddenly Virginia complained of a bad headache and wanted to go home. I offered to drive her and she indicated she didn't want to get back into that wreck. I called a taxi and sent her home. In the meantime, word was out on my accident and everyone was going out to the parking lot to see my car…not what I had pictured for my new ride's review. I started to walk over and talk to Betty, but between the accident and my redheaded date, I didn't think I would be able to carry on an intelligent conversation. I got up to go and looked over at Betty's table. She must have gotten upset because she was nowhere to be seen. Walking out to my car, I must have looked like a kid whose lollipop had been stolen (a real whipped puppy). As I stuck the key in the car door, I heard a voice behind me, "Are you OK…is there anything I can do?" It was Betty.

"No, I'm fine, but as you can see my car has had it." I turned and looked into her eyes.

"Betty, the woman I was with…" She interrupted me, "We're not married or anything. You don't owe me any explanation." I reached out and held her hands. "Yes, I do, because I've grown to care about you in a very short time and want you to know that tonight was the first night I've taken her out. She doesn't mean anything to me."

"I appreciate your telling me that. Don't worry about it. I'm a big girl and I don't break easily. I like you a lot. So does Tim. I'd like us to have something, if not now, whenever. Get your mess together and call me." She reached up, kissed me long and tenderly, and then walked away. Her thoughtfulness at that time is not forgotten to this day.

By Saturday night, I had recouped and was making plans to find another Grand Prix to put my motor and transmission into. I was sure my insurance company would be fair with me, after all I had spent almost $3,000 fixing up the car much less what I paid for it (shows how gullible I was).

By Saturday afternoon, I made up my mind to go dancing at the Wagon Wheel and called and told Bill I didn't want to work. Bill offered condolences on the car. (He had helped me put a cattle prod into the repairmen and kept them honest all the way through the project.) He gave me the night off and said I could get as drunk as I wanted. He would watch out for me. I called Betty and asked if she would go dancing with me. She said, "Sure!" I was surprised.

We danced every dance and found that we both love to clog dance. The faster, the better. The more we danced together the better we got. By the end of the evening people were asking us to clog with them. We had a ball.

I suddenly had an impulse. "Don't get the wrong idea, but I'm having so much fun being with you I don't want it to stop, how about going for a midnight drive. My car is running good and, in the dark, no one will see you in it, so it won't embarrass you."

Betty hugged my neck and said, "OK, my son is over at my sister's house. Let me just call her."

I decided to head for the coast, which was only forty or so miles away. We drove, not noticing where we were, just enjoying each other's company and conversation. Suddenly my heart almost stopped. My fuel gauge was on empty and we were in the middle of nowhere. I brought our plight to Betty's attention and asked her to watch for any place we might get gas. She laughed, "The old run-out-of-gas trick. Well that doesn't work with me. Get a room." Then she laughed again.

"OK, I'll do what I can," I said not too confidently.

I kept trying to figure out where we were when, through a creeping fog moving in, I spotted the sign for the town of Washington. No, I hadn't gone that far out of the way…Washington, North Carolina, located twenty or so miles between Goldsboro and the coast. The motel we pulled up to still had its vacancy light lit. It was 3:00 a.m. in the morning and the man who answered my knock didn't appreciate me waking him up. I rented a room and we went inside. It was a typical fifties-style motel room…everything nailed or screwed down…no TV or phone and fuzzy sheets and blankets. Betty went into the bathroom right away. I slipped out of my clothes and got into bed. I lay waiting on her, thinking she'll never believe this wasn't planned. I had turned off the lights so that when she opened the bathroom door and peeked out, she was able to slip into the bed modestly. The small motel towel wrapped around her body. I had to go so I got up. She pulled the sheet over her head. When I came out, I found the small motel towel on the floor and her starring at me. "Doesn't it bother you to walk around in front of me like that?" Betty asked.

"It doesn't bother me but I hope it bothers you…in a good way." I slipped into bed and slowly brought her body next to mine until the heat was felt before the contact. I stopped when I found she was shaking. "Betty, what's wrong. Listen, just because I got us a room doesn't mean you have to have sex with me unless you want to. I won't hurt you I promise."

"Bo, I know I've been married and had kids but the truth is, I haven't been with many men and I don't think I will live up to what you want. I do want to make love to you, but you'll have to show me because I don't know what to do."

I was hard to believe but true. Betty had never been made love to. I moved her very slowly and patiently. The next morning as Betty and I awoke, she told me that I was the best lover she ever had and that no matter what happened, she would always be glad about the way things turned out.

*   *   *

Working at the radio station, every day I had to sell more and more advertising to see the station barely make money. We went through a number of managers, then one day the owner showed up and I finally got to sit down and talk to him. He mentioned he had purchased a new station in Lenoir, North Carolina, and was in the process of staffing. I told him I would go if he paid me more money. Before the words were out of my mouth the deal was done, and I had agreed to break in my replacement (the afternoon man moving up to mornings), and report to my new job on Monday. Monday was six days away. I went home right away and started packing, during which I tried to figure out what I was going to tell Betty, who I had been seeing on a regular basis. She had mentioned I could save money and solve my car problem a lot quicker if we lived together and split expenses. I had almost agreed and told her I'd think about it. I had spent more time with Tim and I probably dreaded telling him more than Betty.

I decided to tell them both together, so I called and told Betty I got a raise and a promotion and would like to take them to Wilbur's that evening for some great barbeque and also take in a movie. She was excited and had a bunch of questions, which I avoided, reminding her we could talk about it tonight. I had chosen Wilbur's not only because the food was good, but when it's busy (two to three hundred people), it's loud. You can hear someone but it's very hard to carry on a conversation. Consequently, we ate and went to the movie without discussing what I didn't want to...just dealing in the general things like excited about the raise, etc. and so on.

However, on the way home with Tim falling asleep in the rear seat, Betty finally pinned me down. "Well if you're not going to be doing a morning show, what will you be doing?"

"Oh I still will be doing a morning show, just not here. They are transferring me to Lenoir. There's a brand new radio station up there recently purchased by my company and it's a real opportunity." Betty looked like someone had hit her.

"But when…and what about us…what are we going to do?" and then she started to cry. I consoled her as much as I could and left them both crying.

The following days zipped by as I got ready for my move. Finally, Saturday dawned and I had predicated all my preparation for a Sunday departure and the four-hour drive. Betty had called and asked if we could go out Saturday night and I had agreed. We went to "The Wheel" as we called it by now. The placed was crowded as usual. I didn't want to drink too much as I had the drive and all, so I took it slow and danced a lot with Betty. Everyone had found out I was leaving and were buying me drinks, most of which I never touched emptying them in the used pitchers. Betty was having a good time but was very reserved. "Are you packing the car tonight?" she asked.

"No, I rented a U-Haul what with my car tore up. I'm going to leave my car here and I hopefully will pick it up in a couple of weeks. It will give me a chance to see you and Tim." Betty started crying, "I don't see how you can just take off and leave us here. Can't you stay and get your old job back? Things were going so well…I thought you were happy…why do you have to go?"

By this time, she was visibly upset and people were noticing. I went over and paid the bill. "Let's get out of here and go for a ride." I helped her up and we left. I had rented a motel room to spend the night and had fixed it up with candles, snacks and a bottle of champagne in hopes that Betty and I would spend one more night. When Betty saw the room fixed up she turned and looked up at me, "Pretty sure of yourself, weren't you?"

"I had my hopes and wanted to be prepared." She smiled and kissed me. "So did I. Tim is at my sister's."

That night our lovemaking took on a new intensity. I think Betty had made up her mind that if she did everything, I'd change my mind and stay. Even after I fell asleep, she woke me up later on and we tried again...finally falling asleep on each other and paying for it when we woke up that morning.

Breakfast was sad. I told her I did love her and Tim but because of my current situation, I couldn't make the kind of commitment they both deserved and they shouldn't settle for less. As I drove the U-Haul truck away, I watched her in my side mirror go to pieces standing there and it about broke my heart.

*　　　　　*　　　　　*

Lenoir, North Carolina, is on Highway 90 in the foothills of the Blue Ridge Mountains. Home of some of the world's finest furniture craftsmen and companies like Bernhardt-Siegle, Thomasville, American Drew, and Hammary to name just a few. The craftsmen and their families are born, work and die right in that community. Some never have gone out of the state and don't want to. It's a simple life with a church on every corner and a crossroads for tourists heading for the resorts and ski areas over Boone Mountain. The city was laid out on the side of a foothill, so most property was slanted up or down. There were little large tracts of flat land. Finding the radio station was a chore as there were three in town and I didn't know the call letters yet. I didn't know which one to get directions to. My first try was wrong. The second try was golden. "WKGX" was the oldest station in the area and at one time, "the station." Bad ownership and management had let it fade into a dilapidated mess. Old equipment worked intermittently. The transmitter was still the old tube-type so as the weather goes, so did we. Rooster

Bush, a retired postal employee, was "the man" in town. After years of smart investment, he owned one of North Carolina's largest Chevy, Cadillac, Jeep and Oldsmobile dealerships plus real estate, banks, and now in partnership with my old boss, a radio station. Rooster had promised to upgrade the equipment and modernize the facilities. It was getting done painfully slow. That's when I arrived.

My new boss met me at the door Monday morning and appeared to be all excited about having me work for him. (Someone had sent him a tape of my show in Goldsboro.)

He let me know right away that the new format was going to be different than I was used to (modern country), and that he was programming the music personally and it would be mostly album cuts and established favorites. I asked him if he had programmed a radio station before. "No, he informed me, but he had worked for this one for awhile and was looking forward to the challenge. Needless to say, I wasn't feeling very positive about the whole situation, especially when I found out that I would be doing a two-man show with a gospel singer named Steve Prichard (who turned out to be a good friend and fun to work with). Preston had advised me I would be going on the air in the morning and that I might want to familiarize myself with the studio and prepare some material. Luckily, Steve was already doing the morning show and had been for a couple of days, so at least one of us would know which button to push. I met Steve and we spent the day discussing the local color, politics and religion. I needed a place to lay my head and asked for his help. Steve found me a room at a private home owned by an older couple. I had to put all of my stuff in storage, which took me the better part of the rest of the day.

Tuesday morning was an abortion. Having not worked together, we stepped on each other's lines and I started records on the wrong turntables (some would work for forty-fives and not albums. The others vice versa and nothing was marked.) After fighting it for four hours, I was disgusted and thinking of quitting and going back to Goldsboro.

Preston called us in to his office, "You boys are going to have to get your act together if this is going to work. Bo I know you don't know the equipment yet, but you've got to get those record speeds right. Remember the big ones are thirty-three and one-third, the small ones are forty-five RPM, OK?" The rest of the conversation went downhill from there. Weeks went by, and Steve and I referring to our show as the B.S. report (which was never objected to) started clicking. Steve did the local color since he had grown up around these parts and knew almost everyone. I, in turn, had a handle on more worldly things and did the news, law enforcement activities. (Mrs. Roberts' house was broken into last night. The police believe it was the work of a stranger seen in the vicinity, etc. etc.) We intermixed these dazzling dissertations with some jokes and cutups mixed with weather and music. Not exactly major market but apparently acceptable, as the mail started pouring in with positive comments. Preston was impressed and decided if we were so good in the morning, why not let us do afternoons too. In spite of our protests, on we went from 5:00 a.m. until 10:00 a.m. and then again at going home time as he called it (drive time) from 4:00 until 6:00 p.m. needless to say with no raise in pay. Consequently, with our production duties and air shifts, Steve and I had little time to sell and earn any extra money. I found out why. Preston's wife was the Sales Manager and all the good accounts were assigned to her. (You would always find her in the middle part of the day at the local Sonic Drive-In parked in the corner eating or reading a book.) It was becoming crystal clear to me that I needed to be somewhere else. Then the worse happened.

I was on the air around four-thirty one afternoon when Steve signaled me I had a phone call. We let each other know if it was personal or a listener call. His signal indicated personal.

"This is Bo. Who's this?" A very familiar voice said, "It's me, Betty. Tim and I are at the bus station. Can you come pick us up?" My mind blew up. "Bus station, which bus station?"

"I believe the sign said Lenoir. Isn't that right?" She sounded frightened. "Here, say hi to Tim."

Before I could say no, she put Tim on the phone and I was a goner. I told her to take a taxi to the station and I'd pay for it. I was in the middle of a radio show...I couldn't just leave and traipse all over the country...I was angry and upset. Steve suddenly signaled me he wanted to talk, so I opened my studio-to-studio intercom. "What's up big guy, you look like you've seen a ghost." I told Steve about my situation. He advised me to put them up at the Holiday Inn temporarily until I found out what was happening. It was the only decent motel in town.

Betty and Tim arrived at the station bag and baggage. It took the taxi driver three trips to get everything out. "I've left most of our things at daddy's until we can get settled," Betty said. I ignored the remark, hugged Tim, said hello, and whisked them inside the station in time to do the next break with Steve. I had forgotten to pay for the taxi. Betty knocked on the studio window asking for money. The last hour passed quickly with Tim's little face pressed against the studio window taking everything in.

I had called Betty every day and told her how much I missed her and Tim and that I was trying to work out time to see them more, but nowhere in our conversations did coming to Lenoir enter the picture. I loaded them in the piece of junk I had bought when I came to town and headed for the motel. After getting them settled down, I asked her to lay Tim down for a nap and go to the restaurant with me so we could talk.

"What are you doing here, Betty?" She looked up quickly at my tone of voice. "If you don't want us here we'll take the next bus home. I saved enough for the ticket, that's why I needed the taxi money."

"That still doesn't explain what you're doing here," I replied.

"I'm here because I love you and want to be with you and if that means giving up seeing my family, quitting my job and traveling six hours on a bus, I'm willing to do it so you'll wake up and understand how much we love you."

I was stunned and speechless which for me is amazing. I tried to get my emotions in check, reached out, grabbed her and kissed her. "Don't take me wrong. I'm glad to see you and Tim…it just is so unexpected…I don't have a place for you to live and besides, people here are very proper. We can't just live together unless we're at least engaged and soon to be married or they'll run us out of town."

"Well I guess Tim and I will be catching the bus tomorrow."

"Now wait a minute. Let me look around and see what I can find." I was holding her close. The other people in the restaurant had recognized me from the newspaper article and were eavesdropping and giving us the eye.

"Listen, you have something to eat and bring some back to Tim. I'll be back in a little while. Let me see if I can find us something. We'll work this out." Betty teared up but took a deep breath and said OK.

Lenoir was a very small city at that time with little rental property available. I must have made twenty phone calls before I finally had something to look at. I phoned Betty at the motel and told her to get Tim ready. We were going to look at a possible place to live and I wanted her approval. Happy Valley is located halfway up Boone Mountain and was created by a creek cutting its way through the mountain. Finding it was a real adventure. I passed the overly small road twice before we spotted it. It was barely paved and reminded me of two sets of ruts…one going in, the other coming out. It followed the winding creek bed until, all of a sudden, the most beautiful valley opened up—green, lush, and devoid of what appeared to be civilization. One lone farmhouse and a barn surrounded by barbwire fences were visible. I followed the instructions I had taken over the phone and pulled up to the farmhouse. Its red roof and tired front porch, which had turned a weathered gray, reminded me of a painting I had seen. An older gentleman who introduced himself as Leon Schmidt came out the minute I pulled up.

"Well you must be the Bo Wyley I listen to each day on the radio, and who might these two be." I introduced Betty as my fiancé (the pleased look on her face was hard to hide). "Well getting hitched. Glad to hear it. Couldn't have you living here any other way. Let's go out back and I'll show you what I have. Now mind you, it's not much to look at but it's clean and comfortable, probably just the thing until you can get into a house. The missus and I lived in it until we could build this house. (My hair stood up on my neck…built this house. How old is this thing.) We followed him out back and there it sat, what appeared to be the first Air Stream trailer. Its shiny stainless steel sides now gray and splotches of black. The front end had what appeared to be a bay window with curtains. The rounded rear was bricked up, and the stairway leading to the one entrance appeared to be made of cinder block with no handrail. It was probably eighteen feet long and had no central air (something I had insisted on). "What about the air conditioning," I asked.

"Oh, no problem. I just put in a 15,000 BTU side mount unit and that, along with the fans, ought to keep you happy. The electric is turned on and the water comes from a deep sweet well. C'mon, let's see the inside."

As we entered the mobile home built sometime in the late forties, I was amazed…real knotty pine paneling throughout. A living room leading through a small kitchen to a one-person-can-pass hallway off of which was a small closet of a bedroom, and then a full bath followed by the master bedroom which was about eight feet by twelve feet. Not the Ritz, but clean and reasonably furnished which we needed. A brand new side-mounted Sears air conditioner had the inside comfortable and the fan in the hallway sucked it down the hallway. "Remember the electric and water are all included in the rent," Leon reminded us. Tim was excited asking if he had horses and if he could ride, jumping up and down on the furniture. I literally had to grab and hold onto him just to calm him down. "How much did you say this will be?" "Three seventy-five a month with first and last month up front."

I had the three seventy-five but not any more. Well I guess we'll have to think about it. (Betty poked me and slipped some bills in my hand. I looked down and counted four one hundred dollar bills.) Of course we'd hate to lose the place, so I think we'll take it." Leon hadn't seen the money exchange so he said "Okey-dokey. You give me the money and I'll go in and write you up a receipt and you folks can move in today."

We moved in within hours, and watching Tim run around made me realize this was meant to be. The mobile home was set in the middle of a large tract of land and, except for the farmhouse and barn, had an unobstructed view of the entire valley...green, lush and beautiful with the creek winding its way through it lined with trees. With the small amount of traffic, even the sounds of that valley were great. At night, you could hear the creek burbling, the crickets chirping and during the day the birds sang a special song, just for us it seemed. Life was good. A few weeks went by and we were settled in. Betty made the most of the space we had and after getting the pots, pans and dishes we needed, fixed some southern meals that put weight on me just looking at them.

One Saturday after I got off my half-day shift, I drove up past Leon's place on the way home. He was sitting on the porch and waved me to stop and visit. This wasn't unusual so I did, thinking nothing was afoot. How wrong I was.

"Enjoyed your show this morning, Bo. That joke about the pet rock in the piney woods tore me up. Want some ice tea?" I accepted the tea and talked to Leon awhile realizing he wanted to ask me something but was taking his time.

"The missus and I want you and the family to come to church with us on Sunday." (I was an agnostic but good sense told me to keep my mouth shut about that...tell most people and they think you're an atheist.) "Thanks for the invite. I'll ask Betty and see what's planned. We usually take Tim some place special on Sundays. In fact, I think she wanted to go to Tweetsie Railroad." Leon pressed on, "Well if you're so inclined and do go with us, I have to ask you when you and Betty are

planning to get married?" (Married...who said anything about marriage. Oh, that's right...fiancé...marriage...oh, oh!) "Leon, to be honest
with you, we've talked about setting a date but wanted to get settled in
a home of our own first and right now that's what we're saving our
money for."

"Bo, the missus and I don't tell people how to live, but you basically
are living on our place here and that means you're practically a member
of the family, so what you do reflects on us...you understand?" (Boy did
I. No wedding, no rental.) "Well Leon, I wouldn't want to cause you or
yours any problems in the community, so Betty and I will set a date and
let you know when we go to church tomorrow." Leon beamed, thinking
he had just got me off the dime I'd been sitting on, not realizing what a
predicament he had placed me in. I turned around without even letting
Betty know I was at Leon's house and drove back to the station. I called
Steve, who lived near the station, to come over. I had an emergency. He
had just walked in the door himself and told me to give him ten minutes
and he would be there. Steve arrived and I told him of my situation.

"Bo, do you love this woman?" Steve asked. "I guess I do. I'm just not
sure I want to get married again. I haven't been very good at the last
two." Steve looked irritated. "Look, I've seen you with Betty and Tim.
I've never seen anybody else get along so good. You're a family already.
She adores you and so does Tim. You know, if I didn't know better, I'd
swear he was yours."

Steve made up my mind. I decided to marry Betty, and then Steve
came up with the ultimate idea. "I'll marry you two on the air while
we're doing our afternoon radio show."

"What did you say," I exclaimed. Steve explained he was a lay
preacher and could legally perform the ceremony and that his wife
would be glad to be Betty's bridesmaid. All I had to do was get the
license and we'd schedule the event and publicize it on the radio, which
Steve indicated wouldn't cost us a thing and probably would result in
tons of gifts, which it did. I drove home in shock. In the past two hours

I had gone from single, living with Betty and happy, to getting married on the radio.

Betty looked at me as if I was crazy when I told her that's what I wanted to do. "I just wanted us to get married in a quiet ceremony with my family around us," she said. I explained about my conversation with Leon. "So we're getting married so we won't lose this rental." "No!" I told her I loved her and Tim and this had made me realize how much and that I wanted her to be my wife. Betty finally agreed and couldn't wait to get to a phone to tell her family.

Preston, my boss, thought the idea was great and helped to promote it, including a newspaper ad inviting all our listeners to a reception at the Holiday Inn. He had some of our advertisers to sponsor it and they did, providing additional income to the radio station at no cost. I had gotten the license with no trouble and a ring set. I had them made in a couple of days at a jeweler that advertised with us. (The center stone was one of the most brilliant I've ever seen.)

The day arrived. All the publicity had produced a crowd at the station. We stood outside the studio and looked in at Steve, who had the wedding theme playing slowly in the background, lead us through our vows. Betty had chosen a light powder blue outfit that looked beautiful on her. I had the florist match the blue with a bouquet and corsage of white carnations. Steve's wife stood up for her and Preston, my boss, stood up for me.

Tim was the ring bearer and the surprise was that Betty hadn't seen the ring as I had just picked it up that day. Her look was utter bewilderment when Tim reached up to give it to me on a little pillow. It was still sitting in its royal blue velvet box. Although looking like two rings, it actually was one. If you've ever seen a big ocean wave curl, take that shape and flatten it. Beat it so it leaves a natural gold look and in the crevices shadow with black, all to highlight a three-quarter karat single brilliant center stone. Slipping it onto Betty's finger was a moment made for a memory.

The reception was great. We danced a lot and with Tim being watched over at Steve's house, Betty and I had a mini-honeymoon up on top of Boone Mountain in Boone, North Carolina. It only lasted a Saturday and Sunday, but we had a year's worth of fun. That's what Betty and I were about…having fun every day, enjoying every opportunity, stopping and smelling everything, not just the roses. We both had seen some rough times and enjoyed the little times the most.

Our favorite pastime was climbing into that beat up body Pontiac (yep, still had it…even straightened it out a little) and follow the winding creek road to the main highway not knowing where we were going, not really caring. Tim would love it when I raced the engine and asked to drive in my lap. We would occasionally run across a pickin-and-grinnin group of musicians on the side of the road and stop.

Manners still existed in North Carolina. Most of the time we were made to feel welcome and invited to partake of an ice tea or something stronger (home made apple brandy). Some time we carried things along just to have something to share and offer. These times still are some of the best memories in my mind. The secret to most things is the K.I.S.S. principle, "Keep it simple stupid"

We lived about a year and a half in Lenoir. Tim went back to live with his father because he promised him a pony, and he knew he wouldn't be as hard on him about his school work as I was. The day he left I cried like a baby and Betty held me. He had been the son I never had and had always wanted. I resigned my position at the station due to turmoil and internal politics. I called and got an air shift back at my old stomping grounds in Goldsboro. Betty was ecstatic. She loved the weekends with her family and fishing with me on the pier in Surf City. We didn't make much money but we did enjoy life. Then I did something stupid.

Betty and I had been having fights over her spending money on things I didn't feel were necessary. Every time I came home there was a new knick-knack or something she had bought. I would have bought her anything, but those collectible Avon and statues were growing into formidable obstacles. It was hard just walking from room to room without coming in contact with something and having to catch it, or what it was balanced on, to save it. Not an excuse to do what I did, but an explanation of my mental state.

The station manager had hired a new sales associate name Lori. She was in her early twenties, divorced and built like a brick house. Her hair was the color of melted butter and one look at her chest would melt anything. Needless to say, with her spike heels and short skirts, her sales rocketed, which is exactly why she had been hired. I didn't come in contact with her much and actually ignored the remarks the other jocks were making. I had a woman at home who took good care of me. I didn't need any hassle, especially one who I understand had a very, very jealous boyfriend who had already beat up a male acquaintance of hers and had been arrested for it. So, I felt fairly comfortable when she started coming in on Saturday when I did my half-day and some production. She would ask me to cut a commercial for her new clients. This required, or so it seemed, her and I to come in close proximity, as the production studio was small and designed for one person.

She scripted the spots with two voices, male and female, so I had no choice. Even though I did three or four different voices and dialects, I didn't do females and didn't want to. We had been doing this a couple of weeks when she arrived on this particular Saturday with her washed out Levi jacket and tight Levi pants outfit. As soon as she saw me noticing her presence in the station (in which we were alone), she took off her jacket. The blouse she had on was one of those sheer white things that most women wore another lacey thing under. She not only didn't have a lacey thing, she wasn't wearing a bra, and what was visible left no doubt, those were the real things. I had been observing from the studio just finishing up my last record or two…the record ran out and I was so transfixed, I forgot to say anything or start the next record…all I had was dead air. She opened the door to the studio and said, "Well I'm finally glad you're noticing me as a woman, but I think you should start another record before someone catches on." I started the music as she walked up behind me and placed those magnificent specimens on either side of my ears. Her cologne was like a drug as she ran her hands down my chest and whispered in my ear, "I look forward to these production meetings but I have a feeling they are going to be even more productive today." She moved around in front of me and kneeled down under the counter unzipping my pants that, by this time, were obviously in need of relief. Before I actually separated fantasy from fact, she was in the act. Yes, in retrospect I should have pushed her away...I was a married man...but I had given no indication up to that point that I was interested in that type of relationship. She literally caught me with my pants down.

That Saturday proved to be my downfall. Lori and I made it a regular thing and then it grew into even more, all based on sex anywhere, anytime and any way. The passion overtook and startled both of us. We never talked, just lusted and lunged. That was the problem. We had been at this the better part of two months when Don, my station manager, came in and caught us in his office naked as a pair of jaybirds in the act. We got dressed as he waited outside.

"Do you realize what would have happened if someone other than me had caught you?" I spoke first. "Listen boss, it won't ever happen again. I promise. Just give us one more chance." He looked very uncomfortable and said, "You've both been excellent employees, that's the only reason. If I even hear of you two looking at each other during working hours, I'll fire you both. Now get out of here." I knew how lucky I was and said no more, just kicking myself all the way home, not for getting caught but for doing it in the first place. I realized if I really loved Betty, I wouldn't be doing these things. I decided to sit down and talk to Betty. (Brain failure)

The following day I found my suitcases on the front stoop and a sign on the door that read, "Gone to my father's until you're out of here, Betty." I felt like the biggest fathead in the world as I drove away from the house that day. I stopped back by the station and called Don (my boss). I asked him to meet me for a beer and he agreed.

"Well that's the stupidest thing I've ever heard you do. Why in the world did you tell your wife about Lori?" Don exploded when I told him. My reply was emotional. "I knew we were having some problems and thought if I was honest with her, we could work through it."

"Boy have you got a lot to learn about women," Don exclaimed. I told him I was leaving and asked him to get Roger, the part-timer to fill in until he could get a replacement. He asked me where I was going. I told him I didn't know. He said he'd give me a leave of absence for a month for personal reasons until I could get myself back together. We shook hands and he left. I sat and had a few more beers when the bartender told me I had a phone call.

"This is Bo."

"Bo, listen," she whispered and was hard to hear. 'Your wife told my boyfriend about us and he's threatening to kill you and beat the hell out of me after he does." It was Lori. "I'm leaving town in the morning so he won't find me," I said. "Can you take me with you?" she asked.

"Sure, you're welcome to come along, but pack light, I don't have a lot of room what with all my stuff too." (By this time, I owned a blue Oldsmobile Tornado.) "Meet me at the truck stop north of town tomorrow morning at seven. If you're going to run late, call me or I'll be gone…and whatever you do, don't let that boyfriend of yours follow you. I'd hate to have to shoot him."

*   *   *

I had decided to go to Nashville, Tennessee, as I knew many of the country music stars, having done concerts, promotions and interviewed them on my shows. One particular person who ran a major production house in Nashville and formerly had played fiddle for Hank Williams himself, was Jerry Rivers who I had met and talked to a few times. I called and asked if he knew of a radio gig in Nashville. He got me excited right away, indicating that there was an opening night time at one of Nashville's biggest stations, and he was friends with the owners and had a tape of my interview and part of my show. He would call him, play it over the phone, and call me back. I gave him the number I was at and waited most of the rest of the day until the phone call came. "Bo, he loved it. You won't be making much to start, but it's a foot in the door and with your talent, you'll do well. He won't need you for at least ten days so take some time off, get yourself back together and check in with me when you hit town. I'll put you up for a few days until you're settled."

Chapter 16

BETTY CONTINUED

Waiting at the truck stop the next morning was a nerve-wracking time. Lori's boyfriend was known to be a serious person, who under no circumstances was to be taken lightly.

The gray skies and cooler temperature made the situation even more depressing and tense. I hadn't heard from Lori since our conversation on the phone the day before. I was skeptical she was going to show. Seven o'clock came and went and for some reason, I made excuses not to leave…checking the oil again, transmission fluid and brake fluid. Then, of course, I needed sustenance for the trip. I bought two bottles of Jack Daniels from a trucker friend and then an ice cooler that fit perfect on the hump in the front seat.

Miller had pony size bottles out at that time, so I iced down two six packs and the Jack. By this time, it was seven-thirty so I made up my mind she wasn't coming. Just as I headed for the door, I got a phone call. "This is Bo."

"It's taken me this long with my mother's help to shake him. Wait for me, I'll be there in less than ten minutes." It was Lori. Before I could say anything, she hung up. I pulled my car out of sight behind the truck wash rack and waited. A taxi pulled up in about ten minutes and she was in it with four bags and a stereo. I grabbed the stuff, threw it in my back seat and told her to sit down, buckle up and grab something.

Now the Oldsmobile Tornado wasn't a race car, but once you got that weight moving, the big block V-8 gave you all you needed and then some. We left Goldsboro taking the back roads towards Fayetteville. Neither one of us said a word, as I was busy checking the mirrors and looking for cops. I felt we had just robbed something and were both wanted.

Finally, we hit Spivey's Corner (nationally known for its hollering contest), barely a spot in the road and I pulled over to a stop. I grabbed a bottle of Jack and so did she. "Nashville here we come," I said. "Nashville…wow! I've always wanted to go there. This is going to be great." Lori was excited.

The trip to Nashville took us two days and nights. Both of us intermittently got drunk, teary-eyed, then sober. The truth was we both missed our mates and hated the realization. The sex was our escape, so we escaped as much as our time and strength allowed.

We arrived in Nashville around 3:00 p.m. on a Friday. I stopped at a pay phone and called Jerry's number right away. His phone message said back on Monday, so Lori and I took in some shows and danced and drank until we couldn't stand up. I was well hung over when I finally reached Jerry Monday morning. "Hey, Jerry, this is Bo. I tried to call you Friday but you were already gone." "Bo, you should have left me a number. I tried to call you two days ago. There's no job. They called your radio station and someone there told them that a guy with a gun had come down there and threatened them if they didn't tell him where you and someone named Lori had gone. I'm really sorry you came all this way for nothing, believe me."

My heart stopped. How in the hell was I going to get a job anywhere if my former boss and workers were giving out that kind of information. Jerry's voice cut through the fog and made me realize I was still holding the phone. "Listen, give me the number you're at and I'll make some phone calls and see if I can scare you up something to tide you over. There are people out there that owe me favors." I gave him the number we were at and hung up feeling as if the final nail had been driven in my coffin. I went back and told Lori the news. She was real upset. "What in the hell are we going to do for money?" she shouted. Both of us were hung over so I didn't press it…telling her that I'm sure Jerry would find me something. We started drinking again and finally got lost in each other.

I don't remember whether it was one or two days before the phone finally rang and it was Jerry. "Good news, Bo. A friend of mine said he could use you 12:00 until 6:00 a.m. on that big 50,000 watt AM in Denver, Colorado." (Denver, did he say Denver.)

"What about my references?" I asked. "I filled him in and he said no problem. He's familiar with your work. Seems he met you at a broadcaster's convention and you gave him an air check."

"What's his name?"

"Mike Montgomery. He used to do mornings at WCSC in Charleston."

I remembered Mike and knew he would be hard to work for. I thanked Jerry for everything and promised to keep in touch.

When I told Lori we were heading for Denver, she went crazy.

"Do you know how cold it is there? I'm not going to live there. We'll just have to go somewhere else."

"Lori, I don't know how to break this to you, but I'm going to Denver. I need the job." She knew by the tone of my voice I meant it and dropped the subject. I called Mike and he wanted me the following Monday, so we packed up the car and hit the road…again. About two hours passed and we both had said little. Lori finally broke the silence. "I called my boyfriend and told him I wanted to come back."

"I suppose you told him where we were." I asked apprehensively.

"No," she said. "I just asked him about coming back and he said it would be all right, that he loved me and wouldn't hit me anymore."

"I'm confused," I snapped. "You're going back to a man that has beaten you up repeatedly, won't let you have a normal relationship with anyone, and threatened to kill you if he ever saw you again? Why?"

"He's got plenty of money. I can live and have anything I want." That did it. I still don't know where in the hell we were, I just stopped at the nearest gas station and got directions to the nearest airport. I took her there and unloaded her baggage.

"What are you doing?" she asked.

"You want to continue in an abusive situation, that's your choice, but I'm not going to be in the middle anymore. Catch a plane and go back."

"How will I pay for my plane ticket?" she cried.

"Call your boyfriend. I'm sure with all his money he'll arrange something for you."

I left her standing there with her luggage and never laid eyes on her again.

*   *   *

I finally stopped about four hours later and called Mike Montgomery. I told him I wasn't coming, indicating I didn't want to bring trouble with me. I made him aware I had gotten rid of Lori, but indicated she probably would send her boyfriend after me, as she knew where I was headed. I told him I would keep in touch. He wished me good luck.

*   *   *

My mother lived in Eugene, Oregon, so I decided to pay her a visit, but my money was running thin as I pulled into Pocatello, Idaho, one sleepy Saturday morning about eight o'clock.

I had been searching around my dial for a station and found one. KWIK was a small 1,000-watt located in downtown Pocatello (home of the Bannock Indians, Simplot Potatoes and cattle, period). I liked the sound and format so I stopped at a gas station, cleaned up and stopped by the studios. Timing is everything. The owner was in his office doing some paperwork. When I knocked, it was he who opened the locked door and let me in. I introduced myself and handed him an air check.

He very courteously took me into their production studio and listened. He asked if I could do news and I said, "Yes." He ripped some news off the Associated Press wire and sat me down to record. Thirty minutes later I had the job as afternoon newsman and production manager. I worked for KWIK for about a year before becoming embroiled in an undercover investigation of the county sheriff. It seems he was refurbishing all of his old patrol cars at county expense—new motors, etc. When he traded them in, his brother bought them to resell on his used car lot. Needless to say, my story (with documentation from the Clerk of Court's Office) created quite a stink. I was served a subpoena and appeared in court. They asked me for my source of information. I refused to give it to them and was held in contempt of court. My boss told me if I didn't divulge my sources, they were going to fine him $10,000 a day and he couldn't afford that, even though he agreed with what I was doing. I resigned my position so they couldn't hold him or the station responsible. Days later the case was resolved without me and I was released.

Being stuck in Pocatello, Idaho, without a job is scary. Other than Simplot that made fries for McDonald's, there wasn't much of any industry or major retail jobs, so I decided to become a private investigator. The newspapers had covered my exposé and the county commissioners, who I had come to know personally in my news reporting, decided the county needed an investigator separate from law enforcement who could look into things for them. That in itself caused quite a stir. In fact, they paid my contract off after my second investigation. (People were afraid of what I might find.) So, with a little money in my pocket, I opened my own investigative service.

By this time, I had called Betty and we had talked on the phone a lot. She said she forgave me for running off like that and had seen Lori and her boyfriend in town. I asked her if she wanted to come out and visit me. She agreed. I offered to fly her in, but she was too afraid to fly and said she would take the bus.

When the Trailways bus pulled up that morning, I had mixed emotions. I had been real lonely and looked forward to seeing her, but didn't know how she was going to take me not working in radio. She always loved what I did (sometimes more than me).

As she stepped off, I saw she had gained a little weight, but still looked healthy and fresh. As I started to walk over to her, I realized she had someone with her.

"Hi, Bo, this is Sarah. I hope you don't mind. She wanted to come and I didn't want to travel alone."

I gave her a big hug and kiss and welcomed Sarah. She wasn't a day over eighteen and still had some baby fat she was dealing with. It only took the ride home to where I was staying to make me realize she was trouble.

I had always lived at a place called the "Oxbow Inn" since I moved to Pocatello. It was a combination restaurant, lounge and motel with efficiency apartments. Mine was a two-room kitchen-living room, bamboo partition into bedroom type. Brenda liked it because it overlooked the pool.

The first evening back I had the girls dress up and took them to dinner and dancing. Because everything was in walking distance, we could drink what we wanted and not worry about the law. Betty was incredible on the dance floor and we brought the house down when we did our North Carolina clogging. We closed the place and I suddenly realized Sarah was no place to be seen.

"Where's Sarah?" I asked.

"She told me in the ladies room she was going home with this cowboy she had met and not to worry about her."

Sarah didn't have a key so I kind of liked the idea of having a little privacy that night. Betty and I wound up in bed, then hit the pool and sauna and tried it all over again. I didn't have to punch a clock, so Betty and I slept in late. I had very little food in the house, so I took her over to the restaurant for breakfast. Betty told me what a good time she had and how much she had missed being with me. We were just finishing our meal when Sarah showed up looking like three miles of bad road. "Hi, guys. Boy I'm glad you're eating. I'm famished. Those cowboys wouldn't even buy me breakfast." (Cowboys?)

"Listen, Sarah, I appreciated you giving Betty and I our privacy, but spending the night with a couple of cowboys your first night in town isn't going to do much for your reputation. Besides, it's dangerous," I cautioned her.

"I can take care of myself," she said. "Those guys couldn't keep up with me, especially in bed. They had to call for help."

I couldn't believe Betty was in the company of such a slut. I bought Sarah something to eat and told her we would meet her at the room. The minute we shut the door Betty said, "I can't believe she said that, much less did that. I'm sorry, Bo."

"There's no use talking about it. Let's figure out what we can do," I responded.

"What do you mean do?"

"I'm going to assume you want to stay with me out here, am I right?"

"Well we are husband and wife," Betty teared up.

"I want us to try again and I'll try not to interfere because you're not in radio."

"OK," I said. "Either she has to get a job and then a place of her own, or I'll buy her a bus ticket home. You're going to have to talk to her as soon as she comes through that door."

Betty agreed and I left to go to work. Most of my work of late was for insurance companies and lawyers. The cases I was working at this time took very little or no surveillance, just a lot of door knocking and foot-work.

*   *   *

Two months later, my patience had grown thin. Three adults living in facilities designed for a couple didn't work. Betty had taken a job in the restaurant and was making pretty good money. The only problem was Sarah, who had been hired and fired two days later. (Too much time talking to the male customers.) Problem was, Betty left at 6:00 a.m., leaving super slut alone. I didn't feel comfortable about this as she walked around the house all the time with hardly anything on at all. I had asked Betty to say something to her. She did, but it finally took a strong conversation from me to get her to have at least shorts and a top on if she was home around me.

Betty had just left one morning when I heard Sarah apparently taking a shower, which irritated me as she had all day. Why wake me up. She came out of the shower nude and calling my name. "Bo, are you awake Bo?" I pretended to be asleep when suddenly she slipped into bed with me and said, "You just need a little TLC and you wouldn't treat me so bad."

"Sarah, what in the hell do you think you're doing? Get out of this bed right now," I shouted.

"You know you want me. I've seen the way you look at my body," she purred and reached for my privates.

I sprung out of bed, slipped on my pants and said, "Get dressed, you're leaving." "What!" she exclaimed. "You heard me. Get dressed or I'll put you out on the street just as you are." I was angry.

"I have to pack, I have to call someone. I want to talk to Betty." She started crying. "I'll start packing for you so you better find something to put on…now," I shouted.

I packed her up, took her by the elbow, and put her in the car stopping only at the restaurant so she could say goodbye to Betty. Betty recognized I was upset the minute I walked in and she glanced at her watch noting it was a little early for breakfast for me. "What's up? Is that Sarah in the car?"

"Sure is. She's on the next bus out of town so you better go out and say goodbye."

Betty alerted her boss and went out to the car to talk to Sarah. As I watched, Sarah was crying and suddenly Betty slapped her and then came back in. "You're not going to believe this. She claims you tried to get her in bed and she refused, so that's why you're making her leave."

"Betty she came out of the shower and got in bed with me. That's what I was upset about and why I packed her up."

"I know she had this thing for you from day one, trying to get me to let her join us for sex and all…that little lady is sick."

I took Sarah to the bus station and bought her a ticket back to Goldsboro. The only thing she said to me was, "If Betty wasn't around, you would have let me. I know you would." We found out later she not only was pregnant when she left, she also had VD. I might have been promiscuous in my life, but luckily selective.

Betty and I lived at the "Oxbow" for another six months. Then I got the call from Stella. (I had been calling my girls and sending my child support, so she knew where to reach me.)

"I'm in bad health. Robert (her third husband) is in jail for dealing coke. You'll have to come get the girls now." The phone conversation continued but all I heard was I was going to get my girls. I made arrangements to pick up the girls and excitedly moved us into a large unit (two bedroom, two bath) stocked up with goodies and food.

*   *   *

Having them with me for the first time in over seven years was incredible. Because of the time I could take off between cases, I was able to do the things I loved most—movies, swimming, shopping and just simply playing games. Angelique, the baby when I left, was now a talking literate and articulate child. Monique had her mother's looks and manipulative ways. Both had developed into people. Because of the absence, I think I appreciated them more…treated them like individuals. Later they never forgot that.

Meanwhile Betty was accepting and supportive. The girls adored her and, when she wasn't working, went everywhere with her. Betty, however, constantly brought up the subject of me getting out of the investigative business, as it was dangerous and also risky as far as income. Basically, she was right. The problem was finding some other way to make a living. Her solution was for us to move back to North Carolina. After our seventh conversation, I finally told her if you can assure me I'll have a job, we'll go back. That was the wrong thing to do. A week later, I got a call from the Bosley Broadcast Group with an offer to work for them again. An offer I couldn't refuse.

*   *   *

Returning to North Carolina with the girls was fun but short lived. Stella had legal custody of them, came up, and took them home again. Betty and I by now were relocated in Kinston, North Carolina, where the broadcast group had just purchased a 100,000-watt FM country music station that needed a morning DJ. Needless to say, I was back where everyone said I needed to be (except me). Betty and I had been getting farther and farther apart. I didn't seem to communicate to her I needed to get out of the radio business. Every time I brought it up, she thought I was crazy. After all, she pointed out, I was making excellent money. I had the most popular radio show in the area and we had a nice house. I failed miserably in making her aware I was badly depressed and probably in need of some help. This all was obvious when everything hit the fan.

*   *   *

That morning started normally. I got up at four thirty and got to the station by five and signed onto my show at 6:00 a.m. We had just gotten a new very young program director who had insisted on me limiting my ad-libs and comedy bits. He replaced these with a clock plan and music sweeps. At the top of the hour...time, station I.D. and back to music. At ten after…weather, time, station promo and music sweep. Each stop was pre-written on a liner card, which I was to read aloud just as it was written. Needless to say, the station manager and I had a war of words with him saying my way or the highway. I tried to do it their way and my listeners kept calling for days asking what was wrong with me, was I sick. This had been going on for a week. I had finally told our receptionist to put all my calls through to the general manager. This, of course, exacerbated the situation. I got off my shift as usual at ten ready to do whatever production was necessary and then start my sales day until about 5 p.m. When Mr. Pimple Face stuck his head in the door (the new program director) and said I needed to meet with him and the general manager, I knew something was about to happen.

Upon entering the big guys office, I knew by the look on his face he was about to do something he didn't want to do. I had known him for years and although we had a number of disagreements, he was a fair man to work for.

He spoke first. "Bo, we've known each other a long time so this isn't easy for me. Your program director has decided to remove you from mornings. We will, however, keep you as a salesman and production person."

I had expected something, but not this. "When does this happen?"

"Immediately. Your replacement is already hired and starts tomorrow morning," he answered.

"Why am I being replaced when I had the highest ratings in the last survey in this market?" I inquired.

"We've decided to take the station in a new direction. Less talk and more music sweeps. We believe it will, in the end, make us more profitable and give us a better sound," he responded.

The program director chimed in, "Your way of doing a shift is old and tired. People don't want to hear DJ's anymore. They want wall-to-wall music."

"Well if you want wall-to-wall music, no community involvement, no topical comments or personality, I guess you've made the right decision. You definitely don't need me on the air on in production either." The general manager spoke up quickly, "No, wait a minute. You're one of our top producers and now being off the air, you can make even more money." I cut him off. "For who? You or me? The answer to that is simple…you. You've fired me from programming, that means I'm gone from production and sales too. I'd like my check after I pack up my stuff." I walked out of the office with an emotional volcano about to erupt—sorry, anger and desperation. I cleaned out my desk and stopped by the office to get my check. The receptionist told me no one was in, but they would mail my check on Thursday. I advised her to have the general manager call me, as I wanted my money now, not to mail it. She said she would give them the message and wished me well. I tried to talk to someone about my check and commissions for four days and couldn't get through to them. No one returned my phone calls and it upset me to the point of utter frustration. Thursday morning I went to get my money, having left numerous messages not to mail my check because I needed it now.

*   *   *

I had spent the past two days trying to calm down. Betty had helped by making positive statements and making me get out of the house. We had gone to a number of shops she liked. Then we headed over to her favorite—the flea market. I loved antiques and collectibles, so it wasn't long before I got involved inspecting and dickering for different things, which I seldom bought but enjoyed the battle. One thing I did buy was something I had wanted for a long time…an old double hammer shotgun. It had a broken stock and no firing pins, but its age made it a classic. I wanted to hang it above my fireplace (when I finally had one) and enjoy just the effect of it. As Betty and I finished our shopping, I threw the gun in the back of my Mustang and forgot about it what with everything else on my mind. That proved to be one of the biggest mistakes I ever made.

Arriving at the radio station Thursday morning, I was in a fairly good mood. I had made some inquiries with the other stations in the area and found them to be receptive to talking to me. I wasn't especially interested in returning to radio, but it was good to know that the option was there. I, by habit, went to the employee entrance around the side, which required a combination entry on the door and found mine didn't work anymore. Not upset, I walked around to the front where the main entrance, a big lead glass door, led into the entryway. I pulled on the handle and found it locked. Suddenly the general manager came out of his office to the left and spoke to me through the locked door. "You'll have to leave, Bo. I don't have a check for you. As I said, we mailed it and you should be getting it any day."

"I have been calling you for days and specifically asked you not to mail that check as I needed it today to pay some bills. Why did you do this? Isn't it enough you fired me with no severance, no notice and with no respect for the years I've worked for this company?" I was getting very upset.

"Bo, I see that you're upset. You'll have to leave or I'm going to call the police and have you removed."

"Call the police, what do you mean? I haven't done a thing but ask for my check, now open this door. I want to call corporate headquarters and let them know what this is all about."

"I just gave instructions for the police to be called. I'm sure they will be here very shortly so I recommend you leave right now." With that, he turned and walked into his office and slammed the door. I was completely at a loss. It seemed like a dream. I remember shaking the door…walking out to my car…picking up the old shotgun…walking back to the glass door…swinging the gun and breaking the glass into thousands of little pieces. It amazed me that no piece was larger than a quarter. I entered the station and saw the receptionist running to the back. I turned left and stared at the large oak door that the general manager was hiding behind. I thought about breaking that down and then I had a better idea. For the past four days, the station had told everyone listening that I had resigned and decided to do something else. Here was my chance to tell it like it really was. I went to the studio (still carrying the shotgun by the barrel, dragging the butt, never aiming it at anyone). The afternoon female personality was busy with her shift and unaware of what was going on. "You need to take a long coffee break," I said as I walked in. She responded, "Bo, you don't really want to do this do you?" I replied affirmatively and she left. For the next two hours I told the truth about how I had been fired, how radio stations had become jukeboxes and did not serve the community they were licensed to anymore. I let the listeners know the way I felt about the way I had been treated, and I knew my broadcast days were permanently over.

The Sheriff's Department showed up and I eventually surrendered to them. I was thrown in jail, tried to kill myself that night, and months later wound up in a courtroom. I was, because of people who came forward and spoke on my behalf, given time served, five years probation and banned from ever being employed by any radio station again.

I have to say this was the most embarrassing and unbelievable thing I had ever done. I was heartbroken at my stupidity. Betty stood by me through it all, but this ended our marriage for good…not by her choice, but mine. I still communicate with her to this day (she is remarried).

Chapter 17

FAITH

After completely ruining my life and any and all ability to work in broadcasting, I drifted aimlessly for a year or two, did some work for the drug enforcement people and wound up, of all places, in Middleburg, Florida (a bedroom community of Jacksonville). A former acquaintance of mine from my old days in radio had promised me a job selling pre-manufactured housing. Ed had made it clear he would put me up and see that I made good money if I came down. This part of Florida is ugly...mostly scrub pines and old houses. Middleburg is just a spot in the road on the way to Stark (the execution capital of Florida with a large prison population). Most residents' work or their incomes are directly dependent on the prison or Georgia Pacific's big plant there.

The manufactured housing firm I went to work for was located just north of Jacksonville as you came into Middleburg. My friend, Ed, was excited when I agreed to come to work for him. I enjoyed the drive down the coast and was looking forward to the palm trees, ocean breezes and beautiful hard bodies. Boy was I disappointed. Middleburg was a redneck heaven—pickup trucks and four-wheelers. I had picked December to drive down to get away from the cold. As I pulled through Stark in the dark on the way to Middleburg, it snowed. (Wait a minute, snow in Florida? Yep!) I found a cheap motel in Stark and spent the night. I was glad to be leaving town the next day after getting a glimpse of the prison. As I drove up to the sales lot, Ed spotted me and came running up to the car like I was his long lost brother. "Bo, damn you made good time. Come in and have a drink with me. It's after sunrise so it's okay." Well that sort of set the pace for the whole day. Ed's wife, Pearl, worked as girl Friday. She did all the accounting, payroll and basically all the paperwork. I had been out partying with them a number of times so wasn't surprised when Pearl said she had a surprise for me. We apparently were going to the dog track in Jacksonville that evening and she was bringing someone along she wanted to introduce me to. I asked who and she said no one I knew, and remained secretive about anything else. Ed and I spent the day drinking and walking the sales lot so I'd be familiar with the stock. Selling is selling—feature, function, benefit and close…close…close, so I didn't worry about my lack of product knowledge. I simply carried a brochure with me and went step-by-step with the customer. I, in fact, showed my first doublewide that afternoon and sold it…but the credit failed and we had to return the deposit. Ed told me for my first effort I did well. I just needed to do more verbal research into their credit history before I showed them a home (pre-qualify). Pearl fixed us a drink and said it was nice to have me around again. I was feeling no pain when Pearl's secret blind date for me showed up. The fiery red brand new Pontiac "Trans-Am" outfitted with all the goodies and T-top whipped to a stop out front and a very attractive woman in tight washed out jeans and a matching blouse got out. At five feet four and around one hundred twenty pounds with blonde hair and brown eyes, she appeared athletic as she sprung out. The nice tan gave her that extra healthy look. I don't normally try to guess a woman's age, as I'm usually wrong. Later, when I found out it was Pearl's mother, I was surprised. Her name was Faith and she was a bundle of energy although soft-spoken and very ladylike. Pearl introduced us and informed me that Faith was one of the only upper level female management people Lowe's Corporation had (at that time Lowe's Building and Lumber Supply had over 3,000 stores), so I was impressed. Looks and brains in one package. Pearl was in her early twenties, so I figured Faith and I were about the same age. We all had a drink and Faith asked me to show her the lot. She had a home in Gainesville, but was working in the Lowe's store in Lake County. Consequently, she hadn't seen her son-in-law's sales lot and appeared very interested. After walking around and talking for about an hour, we got over the preliminary nervousness of meeting a new person. By the time we got to the track, we were arm-in-arm and acting like me had known each other for years. Later we realized we both felt that way too. It's a wonderful feeling to meet someone and some things click right away, not just sexually, but emotionally and intellectually.

I didn't have enough money to gamble at the track, so Faith asked me to help her throw hers away. She said she always limited herself to three hundred dollars max. We were doing Trifectas and Perfectas. I made her aware I didn't know what the hell I was doing, but I sure was having fun. She hugged me and kissed me. That surprised her and I so much, we let go as if we each had touched a hot horseshoe. Sitting up in the lounge seats you were on display, although no one seemed to notice. She whispered in my ear, "Guess we better save that for a more private moment." I hadn't been in female company for a while, so my reaction was natural and not unexpected. She seemed to be aware of all of my past history, and told me later about her history that oddly paralleled mine. We left the track around midnight. I had ridden with Ed. Pearl had ridden with her mom so they could play catch up and, no doubt, compare notes on me. Faith asked me to ride back with her and even handed me the keys. Driving that new Trans-Am back that night in Faith's company, I felt happy for the first time in a long time. We didn't stop and park, just enjoyed each other's company. The fact that she had more than doubled her money didn't hurt either.

Ed and Pearl lived out in the deep woods just down from the sales lot and had at least two acres of scrub pines around their mobile home with just a pine needle covered road in and out. We arrived a little behind them and found them building a fire outside and some more drinks inside. We all were winding down by this time and sat around the fire in the crispness of what was becoming morning. Ed asked me how I liked things so far. I tried to be non-committal but wound up going on and on about how nice the smell of the woods was and what fun Faith was. (Too much to drink.) I was staying the night with Ed and Pearl, but Faith was supposed to drive on to Gainesville. I was amazed to find that Ed and Pearl were going to let her. When I questioned them about her condition, they said she's done it before, there wasn't any use trying to change her mind. Ed and Pearl left us and went in. "You're not really going to Gainesville now are you?" I asked apprehensively.

"I appreciate your concern Bo, but I've driven it many times and if I get sleepy, I just pull over and lock all my doors. Besides, I have my little friend here to keep me company." She pulled out a chrome-plated thirty-eight and appeared to know how to handle it.

"Well I guess I better be on my best behavior. I wouldn't want you upset at me," I interjected. She put the gun down, reached for me, and kissed me long and hard this time. "I love the way you upset me." She then got up and asked me to walk her to her car. I did and we kissed goodbye. Her hands grabbed my buns and as she got in the car she said, "Those feel really good, looking forward to seeing more of you soon." As she drove off, I desperately wanted to follow her but realized that was stupid and went in to bed.

The following day I thought about how nice that evening had been and wasn't looking forward to spending the evening in that broken down mobile home I had rented in a park a few miles away. Ed and Pearl were going back to the track and wanted me to come along but I said, "No." I closed down and locked up for them. Besides, I had a lot to unpack and laundry to do. A few days passed without any word from Faith. I figured that was that. Pearl called me to the phone one evening. "Hi, how are you?" It was Faith. "I'm fine, but I sure miss your smiling face," I said enthusiastically. "Just my face?" she said laughingly. "Well I don't think we know each other well enough for me to discuss any other part of your anatomy."

"Well we can rectify that. What are you doing this weekend?"

"Actually, I've been closing lately, so Ed gave me the weekend off. He and Pearl are going out of town next weekend," I said excitedly.

"Why don't you drive to Gainesville and stay with me. We'll got out on the town and have a good time."

"If you'll give me directions, I'll be there with bells on."

Faith gave me directions and indicated if I drove up Friday night, she would fix me a good home-cooked meal. Needless to say, Friday night I pulled into her driveway. It wasn't until I saw her home that I suddenly realized that Faith was a very well off woman. Later I found she had over a million vested in Lowe's retirement and had in addition to that, a nest egg. She had played the stock market to the tune of another hundred thousand or so. In addition, she owned real estate. When I questioned her as to why she was still putting in a fifty-hour week, she simply replied, "I enjoy it."

The house wasn't ostentatious, however once inside, the three bedrooms, open family room onto a screened pool patio with marbleized tile and beautiful furniture throughout gave one the impression of quiet conservative taste and style.

She met me at the door in a very casual beach shirt and shorts. As she walked ahead of me, I enjoyed the fact she had nothing on underneath the Indian cotton outfit, which created a movement of free motion that excited me immediately.

"How about you go directly to the master bathroom all the way down to the end of that hallway and take a nice hot bath. After being on that dusty sales lot all day, I'll bet you're hot and sweaty. I'll fix you a drink and bring it into you. Let me know when you're in."

She was right. A bath would be different and welcomed. I rarely bathed, preferring the needle hot showers to rejuvenate me. My mind changed drastically when I saw the royal roman design of the massive master bath. Mirrors, double sinks and a three step up to what looked to be swimming pool center stage, TV, phone and even hidden in the corner a small icebox. I ran the water full force and stripped down, noting the fluffy white terry cloth bathrobe laid out for me on the back of one of the cosmetic corner chairs. As I slipped into the hot water, I noticed the buttons for the whirlpool jets and turned them on full. The frothing and bubbles obscured my nudity, so I felt comfortable about calling out, "OK, I'm in," to Faith. She came in right away, handed me my drink, picked up my clothes and indicated she'd be right back. She returned in a bathrobe and drink in hand. I put this on so I wouldn't get wet scrubbing your back. Lean forward. Before I knew it, she was scrubbing my back with one of those giant sponges. It was wonderful. We talked as she continued and she informed me she had dinner on hold, so we didn't need to rush. "I still have to take my bath. I've been cleaning all day." "Well hop in. We'll conserve water," I said laughingly. And she did. Later in our relationship, she admitted it was the wildest thing she had ever done to seduce a man.

After a preliminary shyness and washing, we had two or three more drinks (hidden in the ice box) and then gave in to the lust we both had been holding back. Faith's body belied her age and because of the maintenance, was soft in spite of a great tan all over (I suspect because of the private enclosed and screened in pool). Her first proud breasts had nipples that tilted slightly upward. Her shoulders were feminine with a petite bone line, yet her musculature was toned and powerful. The walking she had done at Lowe's for all those years had made her buns as tight as ripe melons. She was, to say the least, a sexual feast. One I enjoyed immensely. We had dinner and wine very late that night. I learned then what a great cook she was. Faith and I didn't see anything of Gainesville that weekend, preferring instead to explore each other's fantasies and desires. I am, and always have been, grateful for my ability to relax and enjoy the gentleness and sensation of being with someone who rejoices and revels in our bodies reactions, being able to read the signs that point each other where you are and where you want to go.

Following that weekend, Faith and I spent as much time together as possible. I was making decent money and decided to buy a Trans-Am myself. I invited her over for the weekend so she could share in the experience with me. We had been shopping all Saturday and were tired of the high-pressure antics. I decided to go to one more dealership and then call it a day. As we drove up to this one, it was just getting dusk. The turntable in front showed a special edition wine-colored Trans-Am molested by spotlights. The honeycombed wheels and conservative silver pinstripe decal work instantly drew me to it. Already custom tinted and T-tops to boot, the silver interior showed off it was loaded with all the goodies. As I leaned in to get a better look, I asked the salesman who had appeared out of nowhere, "What's special edition mean?" He explained the car had been customized and a larger computer chip installed giving the big V-8 even more horsepower. I told him to get it off the turnstile and let me test-drive it. He indicated they would be closed in half an hour and we would have to come back tomorrow. I want to buy this car tonight, not tomorrow. Faith took the salesman aside and whispered something to him. All of a sudden, the car was in front and ready. Faith and I got in without a salesman along, which was highly unusual, so I knew something was up. I drove the hell out of it, probably putting twenty miles on it in a very short time. Its performance and comfort were incredible. "This is it, this is the car I want," I announced. Faith agreed and even said it was better than her new one.

When we arrived, the dealership was closing down and the salesman was pacing nervously in front. "Well I didn't think you'd be back tonight," he snapped. Faith asked if the owner was there. "No," replied the salesman as if it was a stupid question. "I'd like to write you a check and take the car with us tonight." Bo will bring it back in Monday for whatever else it needs. The salesman went spastic, grabbing the keys out of my hand and saying, "We don't release cars on personal checks ma'am. It's just not possible."

Faith held her ground. "I believe your owner is…" and gave the sales-man his name. Please give me his home phone and I'll call him. I've purchased three new cars from him in the past two years and had the pleasure of dealing with him at Lowe's. We provided all the materials for his new home. The salesman gave her the number and after a phone conversation that lasted less than three minutes, handed the phone to the salesman. The conversation was short and brief. "I'll have your pre-liminary paperwork done in less than five minutes, but you'll have to come back Monday to sign the rest," the salesman said in a much more respectful tone. Faith wrote a personal check after beating the price down a thousand, and told me I could get my bank to cut her a check Monday. We pulled out of the dealership at almost nine thirty and laughed all the way down the road. The Trans-Am was the first car I ever owned with red interior dash lights, which was eerie but romantic. I thanked Faith for her help and really believe to this day if we hadn't gotten the car that night, I would have been in a bidding war and lost on Monday. They had just put it out on the turnstile that day. In life, as always, timing is everything.

*   *   *

From the first day I met her to the last, Faith was convinced I could do more with my life than I was. She wanted to finance an auction house with me. She encouraged me to write a book (which I did much later on with the help of someone who reminded me very much of her). Finally, she insisted at least I should go to work for Lowe's until I found what I really wanted to do. I finally gave in and made an appointment with her district supervisor for an interview, thinking he would proba-bly give me a department head position or assistant. I was struck dumb when, after a very inquisitive interview that lasted longer than some jobs people have, resulted in my assignment as the new retail sales man-ager for store #254 in Fort Pierce, Florida. Not only did I not know any-thing about Lowe's systems, but I didn't even know where Fort Pierce was. Faith was surprised too, and told me I was the first person ever hired and placed in that management position that had not been with the company for at least two years. To say I studied every available training manual she could find for me is an understatement. However, when I walked into the Lowe's store in Fort Pierce, I knew enough to get by until I could absorb more.

*   *   *

Fort Pierce, Florida, is located about twelve miles south of Vero Beach, Florida, on U.S. #1 and about sixty miles north of West Palm Beach. Located on the Indian River, in 1983 when I arrived, it still had the reputation of a drug-smuggling haven and tough town run by old families with ties to the citrus and cattle business. At that time, they didn't want change, so nothing changed. Today it's a very tourist-positive city…a pleasure to visit. The Lowe's store I worked at was a good day's drive from Lake County. Faith and I tried to see each other, but because I was junior management and in retail, I closed each evening (9:00 p.m.) and worked each weekend. Thus, our time became more and more limited. I didn't date as I was working sixty to seventy hours a week. My work, however, paid off as I was made a store manager in less than two years and it had never been done in less than seven. Faith finally called and told me she had met someone more her age (I had previously found out she was ten years older than I thought) and that she wanted us to remain good friends. She got married two months later. We occasionally saw each other at management seminars and yearly store meetings in north Wilkesboro. Yes, we still had the lust for each other. It hadn't waned. She told me something once that I have never forgotten. "You're probably the only man I've ever been with that I loved so openly and freely that it scared me. I had to release you and settle not so much for less, but different." Faith was a guiding beacon, a beautiful woman and a wonderful lover. I will miss her forever. She developed cancer and passed away less than a year after we last saw each other.

*   *   *

I was leaning over, checking behind a clerk who was supposed to have removed some sale tags on a stack out of merchandise, when her Chanel #5 made me aware of it and I turned and saw an extraordinary creature in a yellow jacket and black skirt standing over me. "Could you help me? I'm afraid I'm just no good at getting the right thing."

But that's another story...

About the Author

This is Bo Banville's second book. His first was titled "Bo Doesn't Live Here Anymore." Bo Banville was born in 1943 and was educated at twenty-two different schools here and abroad. Bo Banville's careers in broadcasting both TV and radio, retailing, private investigations, drug enforcement, and auctioneering with the plus of living in twenty-eight states and spending seven and one-half years in Europe give him realistic insight and humor about life, living and love.

0-595-26430-1

www.ingramcontent.com/pod-product-compliance
Lightning Source LLC
Chambersburg PA
CBHW061349280526
45784CB00001B/197